THE 100
BEST
POEMS
OF ALL
TIME

*In* **The 100 Best Poems
of All Time,**
*you'll find . . .*

### *Lines to transport you to another world . . .*

"Midway upon the journey of our life
I found myself within a forest dark . . ."
—*from* "Inferno" *by Dante Alighieri*

### *Expressions of passionate love . . .*

"If I meet
you suddenly, I can't
speak—my tongue is broken;
a thin flame runs under
my skin . . ."
—*from* "He is a God in My Eyes" *by Sappho*

### *Words that voice our innermost feelings . . .*

"Where is Echo, beheld of no man,
Only heard on river and mere,—
She whose beauty was more than human?
But where are the snows of yester-year? . . ."
—*from* "The Ballad of Ladies of the Past"
*by François Villon*

*more . . .*

***Poems of beauty and bravery . . .***

"She walks in beauty, like the night
Of cloudless climes and starry skies . . ."
—*from* "She Walks in Beauty" *by Lord Byron*

***Words to touch and challenge you . . .***

"What happens to a dream deferred?
Does it dry up
like a raisin in the sun? . . ."
—*from* "Harlem [Dream Deferred]" *by Langston Hughes*

***And verses that will make you smile . . .***

"It looked extremely rocky for the Mudville Nine
that day;
The score stood two to four, with but an inning
left to play . . ."
—*from* "Casey at the Bat" *by Ernest Thayer*

# THE 100 BEST POEMS OF ALL TIME

## EDITED BY

## LESLIE POCKELL

BOOKSPAN LARGE PRINT EDITION

WARNER BOOKS

A Time Warner Company

This Large Print Edition, prepared especially for Bookspan, contains the complete, unabridged text of the original Publisher's Edition.

Warner Books, Inc., 1271 Avenue of the Americas, New York, NY 10020
Visit our Web site at www.twbookmark.com

A Time Warner Company

Printed in the United States of America

ISBN 0-7394-1712-6

This Large Print Book carries the
Seal of Approval of N.A.V.H.

# Contents

# Introduction

I know, I know, it probably seems outrageously arrogant to declare that we, whoever "we" are, have selected the hundred best poems of all time and placed them in this little volume. Who are we to decide what is best among the countless poetic works of all cultures and all times? Well, at least we attracted your attention. But naming anthologies appropriately is not easy. In 1861 Francis Palgrave called his landmark volume *The Golden Treasury,* whatever that means, and there have been many treasuries and collections of one person or another's "favorite" poems ever since. Usually, though, inclusion is based on no better criterion than the collector's own taste or opinion, or that of some other, similarly subjective, authority (Palgrave asked Tennyson for his input). Given the principles on which it was assembled, we feel that this present collection has as much credibility as many other lists of the best and the greatest that have circulated during the recent turn of the century.

Our primary objective in assembling these poems was to provide a small, easily portable volume that would contain the essential works that most readers would expect to find in a book of the best poems, along with some less familiar but equally gratifying selections. To maximize the breadth of the collection, while maintaining a convenient format suitable for browsing through or dipping into at any odd moment, whatever one's mood, we decided to include no more than one poem per poet, in the manner of the thirteenth-century Japanese collection *Hyakunin Isshu* (one hundred men, one work). The poems are arranged in a roughly chronological order (based on the poets' birth dates), from the ninth century B.C.E. to the late twentieth century, and represent virtually every major language group. (Many of the poems appear in English translations by poets with major reputations in their own right.) Most poems included are complete, but several are excerpts from larger works. Some are examples of high art; others exemplify popular culture (we have taken as a byword Stephen Spender's observation that those who try to put poetry on a pedestal only succeed in putting it on the shelf). We have also inclined toward poetry that is best appreciated when recited or read aloud (accounting for the relatively large proportion of lyrical poems to be found here); we hold with W. H. Auden that the best definition of poetry is "memorable speech."

We hope that everyone who reads this book will find it an enjoyable and at times inspiring (or consoling) companion. That some readers may disagree with our assessment of the one hundred best poems of all time shouldn't prevent them or others from enjoying these poems on their own considerable merits, and of course those readers objecting to the selection are free to compile their own anthologies.

This book would not have been possible without the early and enthusiastic support of Maureen Egen and Jamie Raab. Shannon Beatty, Vicki Bott, Amy Einhorn, Jennifer Landers, and Karen Melnyk provided essential editorial contributions.

# From The Iliad

## HOMER
### (9TH–8TH CENTURY B.C.E.?)

*This version of Homer's great epic of wounded honor and vengeance was translated into English by George Chapman (1559?–1634), a contemporary of both Shakespeare and John Donne.*

—ɱ—

Achilles' banefull wrath resound, O
    Goddesse, that imposd
Infinite sorrowes on the Greekes, and
    many brave soules losd
From breasts Heroique—sent them farre,
    to that invisible cave
That no light comforts; and their lims to
    dogs and vultures gave.
To all which Jove's will gave effect; from
    whom first strife begunne
Betwixt Atrides, king of men, and Thetis'
    godlike Sonne.

# He Is More Than a Hero

SAPPHO
(7TH CENTURY B.C.E.)

*Only fragments remain of the lyrical work of this legendary poet, many of them poems of friendship and love of other women.*

He is a god in my eyes—
the man who is allowed
to sit beside you—he

who listens intimately
to the sweet murmur of
your voice, the enticing

laughter that makes my own
heart beat fast. If I meet
you suddenly, I can't

speak—my tongue is broken;
a thin flame runs under
my skin; seeing nothing,

hearing only my own ears
drumming, I drip with sweat;
trembling shakes my body

and I turn paler than
dry grass. At such times
death isn't far from me.

# Psalm 23

## THE PSALMIST
## (6TH CENTURY B.C.E.?)

*While the original Hebrew text of the twenty-third Psalm is usually ascribed to the biblical King David, this familiar English rendition is that of the King James Version of the Old Testament. The translation was the work of scholars who were contemporaries of Shakespeare, and almost his equal in the expressiveness and beauty of their language.*

—⟋⟍—

The LORD is my shepherd; I shall not want.
He maketh me to lie down in green
      pastures: he leadeth me beside the
      still waters.
He restoreth my soul: he leadeth me in the
      paths of righteousness for his name's
      sake.
Yea, though I walk through the valley of the
      shadow of death, I will fear no evil: for
      thou art with me; thy rod and thy staff
      they comfort me.
Thou preparest a table before me in the
      presence of mine enemies: thou
      anointest my head with oil; my cup
      runneth over.

Surely goodness and mercy shall follow
me all the days of my life: and I will
dwell in the house of the LORD for
ever.

# From The Song of Songs
## [Chapter One]

ANONYMOUS
(3RD CENTURY B.C.E.)

*Though the lyrics in this biblical work have been attributed to King Solomon, they were collected in their present form as late as the third century B.C.E. Whether they are read as allegorical songs of passionate adoration of God, or frank expressions of human love, their beauty and power in the King James translation are undeniable.*

—⟊—

The song of songs, which is Solomon's.
Let him kiss me with the kisses of his mouth:
    for thy love is better than wine.
Because of the savour of thy good ointments
    thy name is as ointment poured forth,
    therefore do the virgins love thee.
Draw me, we will run after thee: the king hath
    brought me into his chambers: we will
    be glad and rejoice in thee, we will
    remember thy love more than wine: the
    upright love thee.
I am black, but comely, O ye daughters of
    Jerusalem, as the tents of Kedar, as the
    curtains of Solomon.

Look not upon me, because I am black,
  because the sun hath looked upon me:
  my mother's children were angry with
  me; they made me the keeper of the
  vineyards; but mine own vineyard have I
  not kept.
Tell me, O thou whom my soul loveth, where
  thou feedest, where thou makest thy
  flock to rest at noon: for why should I be
  as one that turneth aside by the flocks
  of thy companions?
If thou know not, O thou fairest among
  women, go thy way forth by the
  footsteps of the flock, and feed thy kids
  beside the shepherds' tents.
I have compared thee, O my love, to a
  company of horses in Pharaoh's
  chariots.
Thy cheeks are comely with rows of jewels,
  thy neck with chains of gold.
We will make thee borders of gold with studs
  of silver.
While the king sitteth at his table, my
  spikenard sendeth forth the smell
  thereof.
A bundle of myrrh is my wellbeloved unto me;
  he shall lie all night betwixt my breasts.
My beloved is unto me as a cluster of
  camphire in the vineyards of En-gedi.

Behold, thou art fair, my love; behold, thou art
 fair; thou hast doves' eyes.
Behold, thou art fair, my beloved, yea,
 pleasant: also our bed is green.
The beams of our house are cedar, and our
 rafters of fir.

# Song 5 to Lesbia

## CATULLUS [GAIUS VALERIUS CATULLUS]
## (84–54 B.C.E.)

*In his brief life Catullus built a reputation for communicating passion with wit and lyricism that has been sustained in every era to the present day. The following translation is by the early seventeenth-century English poet Richard Crashaw.*

—⚮—

Come and let us live my Deare,
Let us love and never feare,
What the sourest Fathers say:
Brightest *Sol* that dyes to day
Lives againe as blith to morrow,
But if we darke sons of sorrow
Set; O then, how long a Night
Shuts the Eyes of our short light!
Then let amorous kisses dwell
On our lips, begin and tell
A Thousand, and a Hundred score
An Hundred, and a Thousand more,
Till another Thousand smother
That, and that wipe off another.
Thus at last when we have numbered
Many a Thousand, many a Hundred;

We'll confound the reckoning quite,
And lose our selves in wild delight:
While our joyes so multiply,
As shall mocke the envious eye.

# From The Aeneid

## VIRGIL [PUBLIUS VERGILIUS MARO]
### (70–19 B.C.E.)

*Clearly influenced by Homer's example, Virgil's epic tells of how the brave Aeneas sailed from the shores of ruined Troy to found the settlement that would become Rome. This version is by the English poet John Dryden (1631–1700).*

—ᴍ—

Arms, and the Man I sing, who, forc'd by
    Fate,
And haughty Juno's unrelenting Hate;
Expell'd and exil'd, left the Trojan Shoar:
Long Labours, both by Sea and Land he bore;
And in the doubtful War, before he won
The Latian Realm, and built the destin'd
    Town:
His banish'd Gods restor'd to Rites Divine,
And setl'd sure Succession in his Line:
From whence the Race of Alban Fathers
    come,
And the long Glories of Majestick Rome.
O Muse! the Causes and the Crimes relate,
What Goddess was provok'd, and whence
    her hate:
For what Offence the Queen of Heav'n began
To persecute so brave, so just a Man!

Involv'd his anxious Life in endless Cares,
Expos'd to Wants, and hurry'd into Wars!
Can Heav'nly Minds such high resentment
      show;
Or exercise their Spight in Human Woe?

# From Metamorphoses

## OVID [PUBLIUS OVIDIUS NASO]
## (43 B.C.E.–17 C.E.)

*This collection of myths of transformations itself transforms unconnected stories into a brilliant verse narrative that has influenced poets and artists for many centuries. The excerpt below relates the story of how the world was created. The translation is by John Dryden.*

—∞—

Of bodies chang'd to various forms, I sing:
Ye Gods, from whom these miracles did
      spring,
Inspire my numbers with celestial heat;
Till I my long laborious work compleat:
And add perpetual tenour to my rhimes,
Deduc'd from Nature's birth, to Caesar's
      times.
Before the seas, and this terrestrial ball,
And Heav'n's high canopy, that covers all,
Once was the face of Nature; if a face:
Rather a rude and indigested mass:
A lifeless lump, unfashion'd, and unfram'd,
Of jarring seeds; and justly Chaos nam'd.
No sun was lighted up, the world to view;
No moon did yet her blunted horns renew:
Nor yet was Earth suspended in the sky,

Nor pois'd, did on her own foundations lye:
Nor seas about the shores their arms had
    thrown;
But earth, and air, and water, were in one.
Thus air was void of light, and earth unstable,
And water's dark abyss unnavigable.
No certain form on any was imprest;
All were confus'd, and each disturb'd the rest.
For hot and cold were in one body fixt;
And soft with hard, and light with heavy mixt.

# Drinking Alone in the Moonlight

## Li Po
## (701–762)

*The first of three great poets who flourished during China's T'ang Dynasty (618–907), Li Po was famous for his romantic poems of escape from reality through imaginary voyages or wine drinking. He is traditionally supposed to have drowned while attempting to embrace the moon's reflection in the water.*

—⁓—

Beneath the blossoms with a pot of wine,
No friends at hand, so I poured alone;
I raised my cup to invite the moon,
Turned to my shadow, and we became three.
Now the moon had never learned about
     drinking,
And my shadow had merely followed my
     form,
But I quickly made friends with the moon and
     my shadow;
To find pleasure in life, make the most of the
     spring.

Whenever I sang, the moon swayed with me;
Whenever I danced, my shadow went wild.

Drinking, we shared our enjoyment together;
Drunk, then each went off on his own.
But forever agreed on dispassionate revels,
We promised to meet in the far Milky Way.

# Moonlit Night

## TU FU
## (712–770)

*Generally recognized as the greatest of all Chinese poets,
Tu Fu lived a life filled with hardship, which perhaps influenced the humanity and compassion that informs his best
work. This poem was translated by the modern Indian poet
and novelist Vikram Seth.*

—⁓—

In Fuzhou, far away, my wife is watching
The moon alone tonight, and my thoughts fill
With sadness for my children, who can't think
Of me here in Changan; they're too young still.
Her cloud-soft hair is moist with fragrant mist.
In the clear light her white arms sense the chill.
When will we feel the moonlight dry our tears,
Leaning together on our windowsill?

# Madly Singing in the Mountains

## PO CHU-I
## (772–846)

*A successful civil servant, Po was briefly exiled in his early forties. This poem, which alludes to his exile, was translated by the great British Asian scholar Arthur Waley, who introduced many of the greatest figures of Chinese and Japanese literature to the English-speaking world.*

—⚬⚬—

There is no one among men that has not a
    special failing:
And my failing consists in writing verses.
I have broken away from the thousand ties of
    life:
But this infirmity still remains behind.
Each time that I look at a fine landscape:
Each time that I meet a loved friend,
I raise my voice and recite a stanza of poetry
And am glad as though a god had crossed
    my path.
Ever since the day I was banished to Hsün-
    yang
Half my time I have lived among the hills.
And often, when I have finished a new poem,
Alone I climb the road to the Eastern Rock.
I lean my body on the banks of white stone:

I pull down with my hands a green cassia
    branch.
My mad singing startles the valleys and hills:
The apes and birds all come to peep.
Fearing to become a laughingstock to the
    world,
I choose a place that is unfrequented by men.

# Rubaiyat 51

## OMAR KHAYYAM
## (1048–1131)

*A Persian mathematician and astronomer as well as a poet, Omar was the putative author of the collection of short philosophical poems known as the* Rubaiyat *(the word means "quatrains"). Edward FitzGerald, using two different manuscripts, assembled and adapted the separate poems into a single work, published in 1859.*

—m—

The Moving Finger writes; and, having writ,
Moves on: nor all thy Piety nor Wit
Shall lure it back to cancel half a Line,
Nor all thy Tears wash out a Word of it.

# From Inferno

## DANTE ALIGHIERI
### (1265–1321)

*One of the foundation works of world literature, Dante's Divine Comedy—composed of Inferno, Purgatorio, and Paradiso—blends religious allegory, political and social commentary, and medieval philosophy into a powerful symphonic poem. In the following excerpt from Canto I— translated here by the American poet Henry Wadsworth Longfellow—Dante encounters his mentor, the Roman poet Virgil, who will serve as his guide to the Underworld.*

—⁓—

MIDWAY upon the journey of our life
I found myself within a forest dark,
For the straightforward pathway had been lost.

Ah me! how hard a thing it is to say
What was this forest savage, rough, and stern,
Which in the very thought renews the fear.

So bitter is it, death is little more;
But of the good to treat, which there I found,
Speak will I of the other things I saw there.

I cannot well repeat how there I entered,
So full was I of slumber at the moment
In which I had abandoned the true way.

But after I had reached a mountain's foot,
At that point where the valley terminated,
Which had with consternation pierced my
        heart,

Upward I looked, and I beheld its shoulders
Vested already with that planet's rays
Which leadeth others right by every road.

Then was the fear a little quieted
That in my heart's lake had endured
        throughout
The night, which I had passed so piteously

And even as he, who, with distressful
        breath,
Forth issued from the sea upon the shore,
Turns to the water perilous and gazes;

So did my soul, that still was fleeing
        onward,
Turn itself back to re-behold the pass
Which never yet a living person left.

After my weary body I had rested,
The way resumed I on the desert slope,
So that the firm foot ever was the lower.

And lo! almost where the ascent began,
A panther light and swift exceedingly,
Which with a spotted skin was covered o'er!

And never moved she from before my
    face,
Nay, rather did impede so much my way,
That many times I to return had turned.

The time was the beginning of the morning,
And up the sun was mounting with those
    stars
That with him were, what time the Love
    Divine

At first in motion set those beauteous
    things;
So were to me occasion of good hope,
The variegated skin of that wild beast,

The hour of time, and the delicious season;
But not so much, that did not give me fear
A lion's aspect which appeared to me.

He seemed as if against me he were
    coming
With head uplifted, and with ravenous hunger,
So that it seemed the air was afraid of him;

And a she-wolf, that with all hungerings
Seemed to be laden in her meagreness,
And many folk has caused to live forlorn!

She brought upon me so much heaviness,
With the affright that from her aspect came,
That I the hope relinquished of the height.

And as he is who willingly acquires,
And the time comes that causes him to lose,
Who weeps in all his thoughts and is
      despondent,

E'en such made me that beast withouten
      peace,
Which, coming on against me by degrees
Thrust me back thither where the sun is
      silent

While I was rushing downward to the
      lowland,
Before mine eyes did one present himself,
Who seemed from long-continued silence
      hoarse.

When I beheld him in the desert vast,
"Have pity on me," unto him I cried,
"Whiche'er thou art, or shade or real man!"

He answered me: "Not man; man once I
   was,
And both my parents were of Lombardy,
And Mantuans by country both of them.

   Sub Julio was I born, though it was late,
And lived at Rome under the good Augustus,
During the time of false and lying gods.

   A poet was I, and I sang that just
Son of Anchises, who came forth from Troy,
After that Ilion the superb was burned

   But thou, why goest thou back to such
      annoyance?
Why climb'st thou not the Mount Delectable
Which is the source and cause of every joy?"

   "Now, art thou that Virgilius and that
      fountain
Which spreads abroad so wide a river of
      speech?"
I made response to him with bashful
      forehead.

   "O, of the other poets honor and light,
Avail me the long study and great love
That have impelled me to explore thy volume!

Thou art my master, and my author thou,
Thou art alone the one from whom I took
The beautiful style that has done honour to
    me."

# Remembrance

## PETRARCH [FRANCESCO PETRARCA]
## (1304–1374)

*Petrarch's poetry—its lyricism, language, and form—has had an enduring influence on the Western tradition. The poem is a translation by the Elizabethan poet Thomas Wyatt, one of the first to introduce Petrarch to English readers.*

—m—

They flee from me, that sometime me did seek
  With naked foot, stalking in my chamber.
I have seen them gentle, tame and meek,
  That now are wild, and do not remember
  That sometime they put themselves in danger
    To take bread at my hand; and now they
      range
  Busily seeking with a continual change.

Thanked be fortune it hath been otherwise
  Twenty times better; but once, in special,
In thin array, after a pleasant guise,
  When her loose gown from her shoulders
      did fall,
  And she me caught in her arms long and small,
    There with all sweetly did me kiss
    And softly said, "Dear heart, how like you
      this?"

It was no dream; I lay broad waking:
    But all is turned, thorough my gentleness,
Into a strange fashion of forsaking;
    And I have leave to go of her goodness,
    And she also to use newfangleness.
        But since that I so kindly am served,
        I would fain know what she hath
            deserved.

### From The General Prologue to
## The Canterbury Tales

GEOFFREY CHAUCER
(1340–1400)

*Although, like all this great poet's work,* The Canterbury Tales *is written in Middle English, its power and beauty, as well as its meaning, are easily understood when it is read aloud.*

—ɯɯ—

Whan that Aprille, with hise shoures soote,
The droghte of March hath perced to the
     roote
And bathed every veyne in swich licour,
Of which vertu engendred is the flour;
Whan Zephirus eek with his swete breeth
Inspired hath in every holt and heeth
The tendre croppes, and the yonge sonne
Hath in the Ram his halfe cours yronne,
And smale foweles maken melodye,
That slepen al the nyght with open eye—
So priketh hem Nature in hir corages—
Thanne longen folk to goon on pilgrimages
And palmeres for to seken straunge strondes
To ferne halwes, kowthe in sondry londes;
And specially, from every shires ende

Of Engelond, to Caunturbury they wende,
The hooly blisful martir for to seke
That hem hath holpen, whan that they were
    seeke.

# The Ballad of Ladies of the Past

FRANÇOIS VILLON
(1431–1463?)

*At once a scholar, a thief, and a brilliantly lyrical writer, Villon has been called the father of French poetry. This version of his most famous work is by the English Pre-Raphaelite poet and artist Dante Gabriel Rossetti.*

—w—

Tell me now in what hidden way is
    Lady Flora the lovely Roman?
Where's Hipparchia, and where is Thais,
    Neither of them the fairer woman?
    Where is Echo, beheld of no man,
Only heard on river and mere,—
    She whose beauty was more than
      human? . . .
But where are the snows of yester-year?

Where's Heloise, the learned nun,
    For whose sake Abeillard, I ween,
Lost manhood and put priesthood on?
    (From Love he won such dule and teen!)
    And where, I pray you, is the Queen
Who willed that Buridan should steer
    Sewed in a sack's mouth down the
      Seine? . . .
But where are the snows of yester-year?

White Queen Blanche, like a queen of lilies,
     With a voice like any mermaiden—
Bertha Broadfoot, Beatrice, Alice,
          And Ermengarde the lady of Maine,—
          And that good Joan whom Englishmen
At Rouen doomed and burned her there,—
          Mother of God, where are they then? . . .
But where are the snows of yester-year?

# Sonnet 18

## WILLIAM SHAKESPEARE
## (1564–1616)

*This is perhaps the most familiar of Shakespeare's 154 published sonnets, especially for its immortal first line. The entire poem is an eloquent appreciation of the transient nature of life and beauty, and a tribute to the power of art.*

—m—

Shall I compare thee to a summer's day?
Thou art more lovely and more temperate:
Rough winds do shake the darling buds of
    May,
And summer's lease hath all too short a date:
Sometime too hot the eye of heaven shines,
And often is his gold complexion dimmed;
And every fair from fair sometimes declines,
By chance, or nature's changing course
    untrimmed;
But thy eternal summer shall not fade,
Nor lose possession of that fair thou owest;
Nor shall Death brag thou wanderest in his
    shade
When in eternal lines to time thou growest:
So long as men can breathe, or eyes can see,
So long lives this, and this gives life to thee.

# Go and Catch a Falling Star

## JOHN DONNE
### (1572–1631)

*Despite Donne's religious calling (he was dean of St. Paul's Cathedral in London), his poetry is notable for its eroticism and sometimes cynical worldview, as well as for its striking imagery.*

—ᴡᴡ—

Go and catch a falling star,
    Get with child a mandrake root,
Tell me where all past years are,
    Or who cleft the devil's foot,
Teach me to hear mermaids singing,
Or to keep off envy's stinging,
      And find
      What wind
Serves to advance an honest mind.

If thou be'st born to strange sights,
    Things invisible to see,
Ride ten thousand days and nights,
    Till age snow white hairs on thee,
Thou, when thou return'st, wilt tell me,
All strange wonders that befell thee,
      And swear,
      No where
Lives a woman true, and fair.

If thou find'st one, let me know,
    Such a pilgrimage were sweet;
Yet do not, I would not go,
    Though at next door we might meet;
Though she were true, when you met her,
And last, till you write your letter,
        Yet she
        Will be
False, ere I come, to two, or three.

# Song to Celia II

## BEN JONSON
### (1572–1637)

*A contemporary and friend of Shakespeare, Jonson is remembered primarily as a playwright, but this familiar romantic lyric may be his most popular work.*

—⚶—

Drink to me only with thine eyes,
And I will pledge with mine;
Or leave a kiss but in the cup,
And I'll not look for wine.

The thirst that from the soul doth rise
Doth ask a drink divine;
But might I of Jove's nectar sup,
I would not change for thine.

I sent thee late a rosy wreath,
No so much honoring thee,
As giving it a hope that there
It could not withered be.

But thou thereon didst only breathe,
And sent'st it back to me,
Since when it grows and smells, I swear,
Not of itself but thee.

# To the Virgins, to Make Much of Time

## ROBERT HERRICK
## (1591–1674)

*This lyrical tribute to youth is reminiscent of the work of Herrick's greatest influence, Ben Jonson.*

—⁓—

Gather ye rosebuds while ye may,
    Old Time is still a-flying:
And this same flower that smiles today
    Tomorrow will be dying.

The glorious lamp of heaven, the Sun,
    The higher he's a-getting
The sooner will his race be run,
    And nearer he's to setting.

That age is best which is the first,
    When youth and blood are warmer;
But being spent, the worse, and worst
    Times, still succeed the former.

Then be not coy, but use your time;
    And while ye may, go marry:
For having lost but once your prime,
    You may forever tarry.

# Jordan

## GEORGE HERBERT
## (1593–1633)

*This apparently simple poem, ostensibly the poet's own quarrel with poetic convention, reveals additional layers of meaning and beauty with every rereading. (It's worth remembering that the Jordan River separated the biblical Wilderness from the Promised Land.)*

—⁓—

Who sayes that fictions onely and false hair
Become a verse? Is there in truth no beautie?
Is all good structure in a winding stair?
May no lines passe, except they do their dutie
    Not to a true, but painted chair?

Is it no verse, except enchanted groves
And sudden arbours shadow course-spunne
    lines?
Must purling streams refresh a lover's loves?
Must all be vail'd, while he that reads divines,
    Catching the sense at two removes?

Shepherds are honest people; let them sing:
Riddle who list for me, and pull for Prime:
I envie no man's nightingale or spring;
Nor let them punish me with loss of rime
    Who plainly say, *My God, My King.*

# When I Consider How My Light Is Spent

## JOHN MILTON
### (1608–1674)

*Milton lost his sight while still in his forties, and this sonnet bears eloquent witness to his ultimate acceptance of this burden. He continued to write great works of literature by dictation for many years.*

—m—

When I consider how my light is spent
    Ere half my days in this dark world and wide,
    And that one talent which is death to hide
    Lodg'd with me useless, though my soul more
        bent
To serve therewith my Maker, and present
    My true account, lest he returning chide,
    "Doth God exact day-labor, light denied?"
    I fondly ask. But Patience, to prevent
That murmur, soon replies: "God doth not need
    Either man's work or his own gifts: who best
    Bear his mild yoke, they serve him best. His
        state
Is kingly; thousands at his bidding speed
    And post o'er land and ocean without rest:
    They also serve who only stand and wait."

# From The Prologue

## ANNE BRADSTREET
## (1612–1672)

*A Puritan housewife, Bradstreet was the first American woman to win international acclaim as a writer. This poem seems to confer precedence to men in all things, but a contemporary reader may sense a certain irony in Bradstreet's defense of women poets.*

—ຓ—

I am obnoxious to each carping tongue
Who says my hand a needle better fits.
A poet's pen all scorn I should thus wrong;
For such despite they cast on female wits,
If what I do prove well, it won't advance—
They'll say it's stolen, or else it was by chance.

But sure the antique Greeks were far more mild,
Else of our sex why feignéd they those Nine,
And Poesy made Calliope's own child?
So 'mongst the rest they placed the Arts Divine.
But this weak knot they will full soon untie—
The Greeks did nought but play the fools and
    lie.

Let Greeks be Greeks, and women what they are.
Men have precedency, and still excel.

It is but vain unjustly to wage war.
Men can do best, and women know it well.

And oh, ye high flown quills that soar the skies,
And ever with your prey still catch your praise,
If e'er you deign these lowly lines your eyes,
Give thyme or parsley wreath; I ask no bays.
This mean and unrefinéd ore of mine
Will make your glistering gold but more to shine.

# To Althea, from Prison

RICHARD LOVELACE
(1618–1657)

*Lovelace was a royalist during the English Civil War, and was briefly imprisoned by order of Parliament. It was then that he wrote this graceful lyric, honoring his love and his loyalty to his king.*

—◊◊◊—

When Love with unconfined wings
    Hovers within my gates,
And my divine Althea brings
    To whisper at the grates;
When I lie tangled in her hair,
    And fetter'd to her eye,
The gods, that wanton in the air,
    Know no such liberty.

When flowing cups run swiftly round
    With no allaying Thames,
Our careless heads with roses bound,
    Our hearts with loyal flames;
When thirsty grief in wine we steep,
    When healths and draughts go free,
Fishes, that tipple in the deep,
    Know no such liberty.

When (like committed linnets) I
  With shriller throat shall sing
The sweetness, mercy, majesty,
  And glories of my king;
When I shall voice aloud how good
  He is, how great should be,
Enlarged winds, that curl the flood,
  Know no such liberty.

Stone walls do not a prison make,
  Nor iron bars a cage;
Minds innocent and quiet take
  That for an hermitage;
If I have freedom in my love,
  And in my soul am free,
Angels alone that soar above,
  Enjoy such liberty.

# To His Coy Mistress

## ANDREW MARVELL
## (1621–1678)

*Marvell's famous poem of seduction is also a meditation on the fragility of human existence and a celebration of the joys of living. It's interesting to contrast its themes and images with Catullus' "Song to Lesbia" on p. 9, and Shakespeare's sonnet on p. 33.*

—⟋⟍—

Had we but world enough, and time,
This coyness, lady, were no crime.
We would sit down and think which way
To walk, and pass our long love's day;
Thou by the Indian Ganges' side
Shouldst rubies find; I by the tide
Of Humber would complain. I would
Love you ten years before the Flood;
And you should, if you please, refuse
Till the conversion of the Jews.
My vegetable love should grow
Vaster than empires, and more slow.
An hundred years should go to praise
Thine eyes, and on thy forehead gaze;
Two hundred to adore each breast,
But thirty thousand to the rest;
An age at least to every part,
And the last age should show your heart.

For, lady, you deserve this state,
Nor would I love at lower rate.

But at my back I always hear
Time's winged chariot hurrying near;
And yonder all before us lie
Deserts of vast eternity.
Thy beauty shall no more be found,
Nor, in thy marble vault, shall sound
My echoing song; then worms shall try
That long preserv'd virginity,
And your quaint honor turn to dust,
And into ashes all my lust.
The grave's a fine and private place,
But none, I think, do there embrace.
Now therefore, while the youthful hue
Sits on thy skin like morning glow,
And while thy willing soul transpires
At every pore with instant fires,
Now let us sport us while we may,
And now, like amorous birds of prey,
Rather at once our time devour
Than languish in his slow-chapped power.
Let us roll all our strength and all
Our sweetness up into one ball,
And tear our pleasures with rough strife
Through the iron gates of life:
Thus, though we cannot make our sun
Stand still, yet we will make him run.

# An Old Pond

## Matsuo Bashō
### (1644–1694)

*Bashō's poem, often offered as the quintessential example of haiku, crystallizes a moment in time just after a frog has jumped into the water.*

Old pond—
A frog leaps in—
Water's sound.

# Epigram: Engraved on the Collar of a Dog Which I Gave to His Royal Highness

## ALEXANDER POPE
## (1688–1744)

*Pope's famously sardonic wit was never so evident as in this brief but pointed verse.*

I am his Highness' dog at Kew;
Pray tell me, sir, whose dog are you?

# Elegy Written in a Country Churchyard

## THOMAS GRAY
## (1716–1771)

*One of the most quoted of all English poems, Gray's elegy links the lives of all of humanity in language that exquisitely balances sound, image, and meaning.*

—⊶⊷—

The curfew tolls the knell of parting day,
   The lowing herd wind slowly o'er the lea,
The plowman homeward plods his weary way,
   And leaves the world to darkness and to me.

Now fades the glimm'ring landscape on the sight,
   And all the air a solemn stillness holds,
Save where the beetle wheels his droning flight,
   And drowsy tinklings lull the distant folds;

Save that from yonder ivy-mantled tow'r
   The moping owl does to the moon complain
Of such, as wand'ring near her secret bow'r,
   Molest her ancient solitary reign.

Beneath those rugged elms, that yew-tree's
     shade,
   Where heaves the turf in many a mould'ring
     heap,

Each in his narrow cell for ever laid,
　　The rude forefathers of the hamlet sleep.

The breezy call of incense-breathing Morn,
　　The swallow twitt'ring from the straw-built
　　　shed,
The cock's shrill clarion, or the echoing horn,
　　No more shall rouse them from their lowly bed.

For them no more the blazing hearth shall burn,
　　Or busy housewife ply her evening care:
No children run to lisp their sire's return,
　　Or climb his knees the envied kiss to share.

Oft did the harvest to their sickle yield,
　　Their furrow oft the stubborn glebe has broke;
How jocund did they drive their team afield!
　　How bow'd the woods beneath their sturdy
　　　stroke!

Let not Ambition mock their useful toil,
　　Their homely joys, and destiny obscure;
Nor Grandeur hear with a disdainful smile
　　The short and simple annals of the poor.

The boast of heraldry, the pomp of pow'r,
　　And all that beauty, all that wealth e'er gave,
Awaits alike th' inevitable hour.
　　The paths of glory lead but to the grave.

Nor you, ye proud, impute to these the fault,
    If Mem'ry o'er their tomb no trophies raise,
Where thro' the long-drawn aisle and fretted
      vault
    The pealing anthem swells the note of
      praise.

Can storied urn or animated bust
    Back to its mansion call the fleeting breath?
Can Honour's voice provoke the silent dust,
    Or Flatt'ry soothe the dull cold ear of Death?

Perhaps in this neglected spot is laid
    Some heart once pregnant with celestial
      fire;
Hands, that the rod of empire might have
      sway'd,
    Or wak'd to ecstasy the living lyre.

But Knowledge to their eyes her ample page
    Rich with the spoils of time did ne'er unroll;
Chill Penury repress'd their noble rage,
    And froze the genial current of the soul.

Full many a gem of purest ray serene,
    The dark unfathom'd caves of ocean bear:
Full many a flow'r is born to blush unseen,
    And waste its sweetness on the desert air.

Some village-Hampden, that with dauntless
    breast
  The little tyrant of his fields withstood;
Some mute inglorious Milton here may rest,
  Some Cromwell guiltless of his country's
    blood.

Th' applause of list'ning senates to command,
  The threats of pain and ruin to despise,
To scatter plenty o'er a smiling land,
  And read their hist'ry in a nation's eyes,

Their lot forbade: nor circumscrib'd alone
  Their growing virtues, but their crimes
    confin'd;
Forbade to wade through slaughter to a throne,
  And shut the gates of mercy on mankind,

The struggling pangs of conscious truth to
    hide,
  To quench the blushes of ingenuous shame,
Or heap the shrine of Luxury and Pride
  With incense kindled at the Muse's flame.

Far from the madding crowd's ignoble strife,
  Their sober wishes never learn'd to stray;
Along the cool sequester'd vale of life
  They kept the noiseless tenor of their way.

Yet ev'n these bones from insult to protect,
    Some frail memorial still erected nigh,
With uncouth rhymes and shapeless sculpture
      deck'd,
    Implores the passing tribute of a sigh.

Their name, their years, spelt by th' unletter'd
      muse,
    The place of fame and elegy supply:
And many a holy text around she strews,
    That teach the rustic moralist to die.

For who to dumb Forgetfulness a prey,
    This pleasing anxious being e'er resign'd,
Left the warm precincts of the cheerful day,
    Nor cast one longing, ling'ring look behind?

On some fond breast the parting soul relies,
    Some pious drops the closing eye requires;
Ev'n from the tomb the voice of Nature cries,
    Ev'n in our ashes live their wonted fires.

For thee, who mindful of th' unhonour'd Dead
    Dost in these lines their artless tale relate;
If chance, by lonely contemplation led,
    Some kindred spirit shall inquire thy fate,

Haply some hoary-headed swain may say,
    "Oft have we seen him at the peep of dawn
Brushing with hasty steps the dews away
    To meet the sun upon the upland lawn.

"There at the foot of yonder nodding beech
    That wreathes its old fantastic roots so high,
His listless length at noontide would he stretch,
    And pore upon the brook that babbles by.

"Hard by yon wood, now smiling as in scorn,
    Mutt'ring his wayward fancies he would rove,
Now drooping, woeful wan, like one forlorn,
    Or craz'd with care, or cross'd in hopeless
        love.

"One morn I miss'd him on the custom'd hill,
    Along the heath and near his fav'rite tree;
Another came; nor yet beside the rill,
    Nor up the lawn, nor at the wood was he;

"The next with dirges due in sad array
    Slow thro' the church-way path we saw him
        borne.
Approach and read (for thou canst read) the
        lay,
    Grav'd on the stone beneath yon aged thorn."

## The EPITAPH

*Here rests his head upon the lap of Earth*
*    A youth to Fortune and to Fame unknown.*
*Fair Science frown'd not on his humble birth,*
*    And Melancholy mark'd him for her own.*

*Large was his bounty, and his soul sincere,*
*    Heav'n did a recompense as largely send:*
*He gave to Mis'ry all he had, a tear,*
*    He gain'd from Heav'n ('twas all he wish'd) a*
*        friend.*

*No farther seek his merits to disclose,*
*    Or draw his frailties from their dread abode,*
*(There they alike in trembling hope repose)*
*    The bosom of his Father and his God.*

# To Jeoffry His Cat

CHRISTOPHER SMART
(1722–1771)

*Smart was a religious mystic whose versification was clearly inspired by the King James version of the Bible and somewhat anticipates Blake, Whitman, and Ginsberg.*

—m—

For I will consider my Cat Jeoffry.
For he is the servant of the Living God duly
    and daily serving him.
For at the first glance of the glory of God in
    the East he worships in his way.
For this is done by wreathing his body seven
    times round with elegant quickness.
For then he leaps up to catch the musk, which
    is the blessing of God upon his prayer.
For he rolls upon prank to work it in.
For having done duty and received blessing
    he begins to consider himself.
For this he performs in ten degrees.
For first he looks upon his forepaws to see if
    they are clean.
For secondly he kicks up behind to clear
    away there.
For thirdly he works it upon stretch with the
    forepaws extended.

For fourthly he sharpens his paws by wood.
For fifthly he washes himself.
For sixthly he rolls upon wash.
For seventhly he fleas himself, that he may
not be interrupted upon the beat.
For eighthly he rubs himself against a post.
For ninthly he looks up for his instructions.
For tenthly he goes in quest of food.
For having consider'd God and himself he will
consider his neighbor.
For if he meets another cat he will kiss her in
kindness.
For when he takes his prey he plays with it to
give it a chance.
For one mouse in seven escapes by his
dallying.
For when his day's work is done his business
more properly begins.
For he keeps the Lord's watch in the night
against the adversary.
For he counteracts the powers of darkness by
his electrical skin and glaring eyes.
For he counteracts the Devil, who is death, by
brisking about the life.
For in his morning orisons he loves the sun
and the sun loves him.
For he is of the tribe of Tiger.
For the Cherub Cat is a term of the Angel
Tiger.

For he has the subtlety and hissing of a
   serpent, which in goodness he
   suppresses.
For he will not do destruction, if he is well-
   fed, neither will he spit without
   provocation.
For he purrs in thankfulness, when God tells
   him he's a good Cat.

# Amazing Grace

## JOHN NEWTON
## (1725–1807)

*Written by the former captain of a slave ship turned evangel-*
*ical minister, the hymn now universally known as "Amazing*
*Grace" (from its opening words) is sung to a melody that*
*probably originated with African-American slaves.*

—⁓—

Amazing grace! how sweet the sound
    That saved a wretch like me!
I once was lost, but now am found,
    Was blind, but now I see.

'Twas grace that taught my heart to fear,
    And grace my fears relieved;
How precious did that grace appear
    The hour I first believed.

Through many dangers, toils, and snares
    I have already come;
'Tis grace hath brought me safe thus far,
    And grace will lead me home.

The Lord has promised good to me,
    His word my hope secures;
He will my shield and portion be
    As long as life endures.

# Tyger! Tyger!

## WILLIAM BLAKE
## (1757–1827)

*This poem has often been taken as an attack on the soullessness of the Industrial Revolution, but it carries a deeper resonance as a mystical parable of the dark side of human nature.*

—ɯ—

Tyger! Tyger! burning bright
In the forests of the night,
What immortal hand or eye
Could frame thy fearful symmetry?

In what distant deeps or skies
Burnt the fire of thine eyes?
On what wings dare he aspire?
What the hand dare seize the fire?

And what shoulder, and what art,
Could twist the sinews of thy heart?
And when thy heart began to beat,
What dread hand? and what dread feet?

What the hammer? what the chain?
In what furnace was thy brain?
What the anvil? what dread grasp
Dare its deadly terrors clasp?

When the stars threw down their spears,
And watered heaven with their tears,
Did he smile his work to see?
Did he who made the Lamb make thee?

Tyger! Tyger! burning bright
In the forests of the night,
What immortal hand or eye
Dare frame thy fearful symmetry?

# To a Mouse

## ROBERT BURNS
### (1759–1796)

*Although Burns wrote in Scottish dialect, the wit and warm humanity of his verse has insured its enduring popularity for over two centuries.*

—ɯ—

Wee, sleeket, cowran, tim'rous beastie,
   O, what panic's in thy breastie!
Thou need na start awa sae hasty,
   Wi' bickering brattle!
I wad be laith to rin an' chase thee,
   Wi' murd'ring pattle!

   I'm truly sorry Man's dominion
Has broken Nature's social union,
   An' justifies that ill opinion,
   Which makes thee startle,
At me, thy poor, earth-born companion,
   An' fellow-mortal!

I doubt na, whyles, but thou may thieve;
What then? poor beastie, thou maun live!
   A daimen-icker in a thrave
     'S a sma' request:
   I'll get a blessin wi' the lave,
     An' never miss't!

Thy wee-bit housie, too, in ruin!
It's silly wa's the win's are strewin!
An' naething, now, to big a new ane,
O' foggage green!
An' bleak December's winds ensuin,
Baith snell an' keen!

Thou saw the fields laid bare an' wast,
An' weary Winter comin fast,
An' cozie here, beneath the blast,
Thou thought to dwell,
Till crash! the cruel coulter past
Out thro' thy cell.

That wee-bit heap o' leaves an' stibble,
Has cost thee monie a weary nibble!
Now thou's turn'd out, for a' thy trouble,
But house or hald.
To thole the Winter's sleety dribble,
An' cranreuch cauld!

But Mousie, thou are no thy-lane,
In proving foresight may be vain:
The best laid schemes o' Mice an' Men,
Gang aft agley,
An' lea'e us nought but grief an' pain,
For promis'd joy!

Still, thou art blest, compar'd wi' me!
The present only toucheth thee:
But Och! I backward cast my e'e,
On prospects drear!
An' forward, tho' I canna see,
I guess an' fear!

# Ode to Joy

## FRIEDRICH VON SCHILLER
## (1759–1805)

*This stirring expression of Romanticism by one of Germany's greatest literary figures provides the lyrics for the final movement of Beethoven's Ninth Symphony.*

—ᴍ—

O friends, no more these sounds!
Let us sing more cheerful songs,
More full of joy!

Joy, bright spark of divinity,
Daughter of Elysium,
Fire-inspired we tread
Thy sanctuary
Thy magic power re-united
All that custom has divided
All men become brothers
Under the sway of thy gentle wings.

Whoever has created
An abiding friendship,
Or has won
A true and loving wife,
All who can call at least one soul theirs,

Join in our song of praise;
But any who cannot must creep tearfully
Away from our circle.

All creatures drink of joy
At nature's breast.
Just and unjust
Alike taste of her gift;
She gave us kisses and the fruit of the vine,
A tried friend to the end.
Even the worm can feel contentment,
And the cherub stands before God!

Gladly, like the heavenly bodies
Which He set on their courses
Through the splendor of the firmament;
Thus, brothers, you should run your race,
As a hero going to conquest.

You millions, I embrace you.
This kiss is for all the world!
Brothers, above the starry canopy
There must dwell a loving Father.
Do you fall in worship, you millions?
World, do you know your Creator?
Seek Him in the heavens;
Above the stars must He dwell.

# Don't Kill that Fly!

## KOBAYASHI ISSA
## (1763–1827)

*Issa's haiku are notable for their sympathetic treatment of everyday objects.*

Look, don't kill that fly!
It is making a prayer to you
By rubbing its hands and feet.

# The World Is Too Much with Us

WILLIAM WORDSWORTH
(1770–1850)

*Considered the greatest writer of sonnets in English after Shakespeare and Milton, Wordsworth unites in this poem disdain for modern life, an almost ecstatic vision of the beauties of nature, and a nostalgic yearning for a mythical golden age.*

—m—

The world is too much with us; late and soon,
Getting and spending, we lay waste our
     powers:
Little we see in Nature that is ours;
We have given our hearts away, a sordid boon!
The Sea that bares her bosom to the moon;
The winds that will be howling at all hours,
And are up-gathered now like sleeping
     flowers;
For this, for everything, we are out of tune;
It moves us not.—Great God! I'd rather be
A Pagan suckled in a creed outworn;
So might I, standing on this pleasant lea,
Have glimpses that would make me less
     forlorn;
Have sight of Proteus rising from the sea;
Or hear old Triton blow his wreathed horn.

# From The Lay of the Last Minstrel

## WALTER SCOTT
## (1771–1832)

*Although today Scott is best known for his historical novels, including* Ivanhoe, *his reputation was established in 1805 with the full-length narrative poem* The Lay of the Last Minstrel. *This excerpt from it has long been regarded as a classic evocation of patriotism.*

—❧—

Breathes there the man with soul so dead,
Who never to himself hath said,
"This is my own, my native land!"
Whose heart hath ne'er within him burn'd
As home his footsteps he hath turn'd
From wandering on a foreign strand?
If such there breathe, go, mark him well;
For him no Minstrel raptures swell;
High though his titles, proud his name,
Boundless his wealth as wish can claim;
Despite those titles, power, and pelf,
The wretch, concentred all in self,
Living, shall forfeit fair renown,
And, doubly dying, shall go down
To the vile dust from whence he sprung,
Unwept, unhonor'd, and unsung.

# Kubla Khan

## SAMUEL TAYLOR COLERIDGE
## (1772–1834)

*Supposedly written after Coleridge was awakened from an opium-drugged sleep, "Kubla Khan" is often seen as a brilliant fragment of a lost vision, but its ending can also be read as an awed comment on the uncanny phenomenon of creative genius.*

In Xanadu did Kubla Khan
A stately pleasure-dome decree:
Where Alph, the sacred river, ran
Through caverns measureless to man
Down to a sunless sea.
So twice five miles of fertile ground
With walls and towers were girdled round:
And there were gardens bright with sinuous
    rills,
Where blossomed many an incense-bearing
    tree;
And here were forests ancient as the hills,
Enfolding sunny spots of greenery.

But oh! that deep romantic chasm which
    slanted
Down the green hill athwart a cedarn cover!

A savage place! as holy and enchanted
As e'er beneath a waning moon was haunted
By woman wailing for her demon-lover!
And from this chasm, with ceaseless turmoil
    seething,
As if this earth in fast thick pants were
    breathing,
A mighty fountain momently was forced:
Amid whose swift half-intermitted burst
Huge fragments vaulted like rebounding hail,
Or chaffy grain beneath the thresher's flail:
And 'mid these dancing rocks at once and
    ever
It flung up momently the sacred river.
Five miles meandering with a mazy motion
Through wood and dale the sacred river ran,
Then reached the caverns measureless to
    man,
And sank in tumult to a lifeless ocean:
And 'mid this tumult Kubla heard from far
Ancestral voices prophesying war!

The shadow of the dome of pleasure
Floated midway on the waves;
Where was heard the mingled measure
From the fountain and the caves.
It was a miracle of rare device,
A sunny pleasure-dome with caves of ice!
A damsel with a dulcimer

In a vision once I saw:
It was an Abyssinian maid,
And on her dulcimer she played,
Singing of Mount Abora.
Could I revive within me
Her symphony and song,
To such a deep delight 'twould win me,
That with music loud and long,
I would build that dome in air,
That sunny dome! those caves of ice!
And all who heard should see them there,
And all should cry, Beware! Beware!
His flashing eyes, his floating hair!
Weave a circle round him thrice,
And close your eyes with holy dread,
For he on honey-dew hath fed,
And drunk the milk of Paradise.

# A Visit from St. Nicholas

CLEMENT CLARKE MOORE
(1779–1863)

*Moore wrote this narrative poem for his own children, but its anonymous publication soon made it a Christmas classic.*

—ᴍ—

'Twas the night before Christmas when all
     through the house
Not a creature was stirring, not even a mouse;
The stockings were hung by the chimney with
     care,
In hopes that St. Nicholas soon would be there.
The children were nestled all snug in their beds,
While visions of sugar-plums danced in their
     heads;

Mamma in her 'kerchief, and I in my cap,
Had just settled down for a long winter's nap,
When out on the lawn there arose such a
     clatter,
I sprang from the bed to see what was the
     matter.
Away to the window I flew like a flash,
Tore open the shutters and threw up the sash.

The moon on the breast of the new-fallen snow
Gave the lustre of midday to objects below,
When, what to my wondering eyes should
        appear,
But a miniature sleigh, and eight tiny reindeer,
With a little old driver, so lively and quick,
I knew in a moment it must be St. Nick.

More rapid than eagles his coursers they came,
And he whistled, and shouted, and called
        them by name;
"Now, Dasher! Now, Dancer! Now, Prancer
        and Vixen!
On, Comet! on, Cupid! on, Donner and Blitzen!
To the top of the porch! to the top of the wall!
Now dash away! dash away! dash away all!"

As dry leaves that before the wild hurricane fly,
When they meet with an obstacle, mount to
        the sky,
So up to the house-top the coursers they flew,
With the sleigh full of toys, and St. Nicholas
        too.
And then, in a twinkling, I heard on the roof
The prancing and pawing of each little hoof.
As I drew in my hand, and was turning around,
Down the chimney St. Nicholas came with a
        bound.

He was dressed all in fur, from his head to his
     foot,
And his clothes were all tarnished with ashes
     and soot;
A bundle of toys he had flung on his back,
And he looked like a peddler just opening his
     pack.
His eyes—how they twinkled! his dimples how
     merry!
His cheeks were like roses, his nose like a
     cherry!
His droll little mouth was drawn up like a bow,
And the beard of his chin was as white as the
     snow;
The stump of a pipe he held tight in his teeth,
And the smoke it encircled his head like a
     wreath;
He had a broad face and a little round belly,
That shook when he laughed like a bowlful of
     jelly.
He was chubby and plump, a right jolly old elf,
And I laughed when I saw him, in spite of myself;

A wink of his eye and a twist of his head,
Soon gave me to know I had nothing to dread;
He spoke not a word, but went straight to his
     work,
And filled all the stockings; then turned with a
     jerk,

And laying his finger aside of his nose,
And giving a nod, up the chimney he rose;
He sprang to his sleigh, to his team gave a
    whistle,
And away they all flew like the down of a thistle.
But I heard him exclaim, ere he drove out of
    sight,

"HAPPY CHRISTMAS TO ALL,
AND TO ALL A GOOD NIGHT!"

# Abou Ben Adhem

## LEIGH HUNT
## (1784–1859)

*While predominantly known for his journalism and the creation of several periodicals, Hunt also wrote poetry. "Abou Ben Adhem" is a dramatic piece expressing a humanistic philosophy.*

—⚇—

Abou Ben Adhem (may his tribe increase!)
Awoke one night from a deep dream of
     peace,
And saw, within the moonlight in his room,
Making it rich, and like a lily in bloom,
An angel writing in a book of gold:—
Exceeding peace had made Ben Adhem bold,
And to the presence in the room he said,
"What writest thou?"—The vision raised its
     head,
And with a look made of all sweet accord,
Answered, "The names of those who love the
     Lord."
"And is mine one?" said Abou. "Nay, not so,"
Replied the angel. Abou spoke more low,
But cheerly still; and said, "I pray thee, then,
Write me as one that loves his fellow men."

The angel wrote, and vanished. The next night
It came again with a great wakening light,
And showed the names whom love of God
     had blest,
And lo! Ben Adhem's name led all the rest.

# She Walks in Beauty

## LORD BYRON
### (1788–1824)

*Written to be set to traditional Jewish music, "She Walks in Beauty" was Byron's elaborate compliment the morning after meeting a beautiful woman.*

—⚬⚬⚬—

She walks in beauty, like the night
    Of cloudless climes and starry skies;
And all that's best of dark and bright
    Meet in her aspect and her eyes:
Thus mellow'd to that tender light
    Which heaven to gaudy day denies.

One shade the more, one ray the less,
    Had half impair'd the nameless grace
Which waves in every raven tress,
    Or softly lightens o'er her face;
Where thoughts serenely sweet express
    How pure, how dear their dwelling-place.

And on that cheek, and o'er that brow,
    So soft, so calm, yet eloquent,
The smiles that win, the tints that glow,
    But tell of days in goodness spent,
A mind at peace with all below,
    A heart whose love is innocent!

# Ozymandias

## PERCY BYSSHE SHELLEY
### (1792–1822)

*Shelley's poem about King Ozymandias is an ironic comment on a once great figure whose only lasting legacy is a ruined monument in the sand.*

—ᨑ—

I met a traveler from an antique land
Who said: Two vast and trunkless legs of stone
Stand in the desert. Near them, on the sand,
Half sunk, a shattered visage lies, whose frown,
And wrinkled lip, and sneer of cold command,
Tell that its sculptor well those passions read
Which yet survive, stamped on these lifeless
      things,
The hand that mocked them, and the heart
      that fed;
And on the pedestal these words appear:
"My name is Ozymandias, king of kings:
Look on my works, ye Mighty, and despair!"
Nothing beside remains. Round the decay
Of that colossal wreck, boundless and bare
The lone and level sands stretch far away.

# Thanatopsis

## WILLIAM CULLEN BRYANT
## (1794–1878)

*Written when its author was seventeen years old,
"Thanatopsis" (the title means "view of death") is both a
great poem of consolation and a majestic meditation on
humankind's intimate relationship with the rest of nature.*

—⚊⚊—

To him who, in the love of Nature, holds
Communion with her visible forms, she speaks
A various language: for his gayer hours
She has a voice of gladness, and a smile
And eloquence of beauty; and she glides
Into his darker musings, with a mild
And healing sympathy, that steals away
Their sharpness, ere he is aware. When thoughts
Of the last bitter hour come like a blight
Over thy spirit, and sad images
Of the stern agony, and shroud, and pall,
And breathless darkness, and the narrow house
Make thee to shudder, and grow sick at heart,—
Go forth under the open sky, and list
To Nature's teachings, while from all around—
Earth and her waters, and the depths of air—
Comes a still voice:—Yet a few days, and thee
The all-beholding sun shall see no more

In all his course; nor yet in the cold ground,
Where thy pale form was laid, with many tears,
Nor in the embrace of ocean, shall exist
Thy image. Earth, that nourished thee, shall claim
Thy growth, to be resolved to earth again;
And, lost each human trace, surrendering up
Thine individual being, shalt thou go
To mix forever with the elements;
To be a brother to the insensible rock,
And to the sluggish clod, which the rude swain
Turns with his share, and treads upon. The oak
Shall send his roots abroad, and pierce thy
    mold.
Yet not to thine eternal resting place
Shalt thou retire alone—nor couldst thou wish
Couch more magnificent. Thou shalt lie down
With patriarchs of the infant world—with kings,
The powerful of the earth—the wise, the good,
Fair forms, and hoary seers of ages past,
All in one mighty sepulcher. The hills,
Rock-ribbed, and ancient as the sun; the vales
Stretching in pensive quietness between;
The venerable woods; rivers that move
In majesty, and the complaining brooks,
That make the meadows green; and, poured
    round all
Old ocean's gray and melancholy waste—
Are but the solemn decorations all
Of the great tomb of man! The golden sun,

The planets, all the infinite host of heaven,
Are shining on the sad abodes of death,
Through the still lapse of ages. All that tread
The globe are but a handful to the tribes
That slumber in its bosom. Take the wings
Of morning, pierce the Barcan wilderness,
Or lose thyself in the continuous woods
Where rolls the Oregon and hears no sound
Save his own dashings—yet the dead are there;
And millions in those solitudes, since first
The flight of years began, have laid them down
In their last sleep—the dead reign there alone!
So shalt thou rest, and what if thou withdraw
In silence from the living; and no friend
Take note of thy departure? All that breathe
Will share thy destiny. The gay will laugh
When thou art gone, the solemn brood of care
Plod on, and each one as before shall chase
His favorite phantom; yet all these shall leave
Their mirth and their employments, and shall
    come
And make their bed with thee. As the long train
Of ages glides away, the sons of men—
The youth in life's green spring, and he who goes
In the full strength of years, matron and maid,
And the sweet babe, and the gray-headed
    man—
Shall one by one be gathered to thy side,
By those, who in their turn shall follow them.

So live that when thy summons comes to join
The innumerable caravan that moves
To that mysterious realm, where each shall
    take
His chamber in the silent halls of death,
Thou go not, like the quarry slave at night,
Scourged to his dungeon, but, sustained and
    soothed
By an unfaltering trust, approach thy grave
Like one who wraps the drapery of his couch
About him, and lies down to pleasant dreams.

# Ode on a Grecian Urn

## JOHN KEATS
## (1795–1821)

*In this poem, Keats meditates on a typical Romantic senti-
ment espousing the belief that art and beauty transcend
the real world.*

—〰—

Thou still unravish'd bride of quietness,
   Thou foster-child of silence and slow time,
Sylvan historian, who canst thus express
   A flowery tale more sweetly than our rhyme:
What leaf-fring'd legend haunts about thy shape
   Of deities or mortals, or of both,
      In Tempe or the dales of Arcady?
   What men or gods are these? What
         maidens loth?
What mad pursuit? What struggle to escape?
   What pipes and timbrels? What wild ecstasy?

Heard melodies are sweet, but those unheard
   Are sweeter; therefore, ye soft pipes, play on;
Not to the sensual ear, but, more endear'd,
   Pipe to the spirit ditties of no tone:
Fair youth, beneath the trees, thou canst not leave
   Thy song, nor ever can those trees be bare;
      Bold Lover, never, never canst thou kiss,

Though winning near the goal yet, do not grieve;
  She cannot fade, though thou hast not thy
      bliss,
    For ever wilt thou love, and she be fair!

Ah, happy, happy boughs! that cannot shed
  Your leaves, nor ever bid the Spring adieu;
And, happy melodist, unwearied,
  For ever piping songs for ever new;
More happy love! more happy, happy love!
  For ever warm and still to be enjoy'd,
    For ever panting, and for ever young;
All breathing human passion far above,
  That leaves a heart high-sorrowful and
      cloy'd,
    A burning forehead, and a parching
      tongue.

Who are these coming to the sacrifice?
  To what green altar, O mysterious priest,
Lead'st thou that heifer lowing at the skies,
  And all her silken flanks with garlands
      drest?
What little town by river or sea shore,
  Or mountain-built with peaceful citadel,
    Is emptied of this folk, this pious morn?
And, little town, thy streets for evermore
  Will silent be; and not a soul to tell
    Why thou art desolate, can e'er return.

O Attic shape! Fair attitude! with brede
  Of marble men and maidens overwrought,
With forest branches and the trodden weed;
  Thou, silent form, dost tease us out of
      thought
As doth eternity: Cold Pastoral!
  When old age shall this generation waste,
    Thou shalt remain, in midst of other woe
Than ours, a friend to man, to whom thou say'st,
  "Beauty is truth, truth beauty,—that is all
    Ye know on earth, and all ye need to
      know."

# Concord Hymn

## RALPH WALDO EMERSON
## (1803–1882)

*The Battle of Concord precipitated the American Revolutionary War. The commemorative "Concord Hymn" was first recited on July 4, 1837, upon completion of the Concord Monument.*

—ᴍ—

By the rude bridge that arched the flood,
Their flag to April's breeze unfurled,
Here once the embattled farmers stood,
And fired the shot heard round the world.

The foe long since in silence slept;
Alike the conqueror silent sleeps;
And Time the ruined bridge has swept
Down the dark stream which seaward creeps.

On this green bank, by this soft stream,
We set today a votive stone;
That memory may their deed redeem,
When, like our sires, our sons are gone.

Spirit, that made those heroes dare
To die, or leave their children free,
Bid Time and Nature gently spare
The shaft we raise to them and thee.

# How Do I Love Thee?

## ELIZABETH BARRETT BROWNING
### (1806–1861)

*The poet wrote this, one of her* Sonnets from the Portuguese, *to her soon-to-be-husband, Robert Browning, during their celebrated courtship.*

—❦—

How do I love thee? Let me count the ways.
I love thee to the depth and breadth and height
My soul can reach, when feeling out of sight
For the ends of Being and ideal Grace.
I love thee to the level of every day's
Most quiet need, by sun and candlelight.
I love thee freely, as men strive for Right;
I love thee purely, as they turn from Praise.
I love with a passion put to use
In my old griefs, and with my childhood's faith.
I love thee with a love I seemed to lose
With my lost saints,—I love thee with the breath,
Smiles, tears, of all my life!—and, if God choose,
I shall but love thee better after death.

# Paul Revere's Ride

## HENRY WADSWORTH LONGFELLOW
### (1807–1882)

*One of America's most beloved poets, Longfellow was renowned for writing verse with an infectious songlike meter and rhyme scheme, as exemplified by this poem, based on a legendary event in American history.*

—∿—

Listen my children and you shall hear
Of the midnight ride of Paul Revere,
On the eighteenth of April, in Seventy-five;
Hardly a man is now alive
Who remembers that famous day and year.

He said to his friend, "If the British march
By land or sea from the town tonight,
Hang a lantern aloft in the belfry arch
Of the North Church tower as a signal light,—
One if by land, and two if by sea;
And I on the opposite shore will be,
Ready to ride and spread the alarm
Through every Middlesex village and farm,
For the country folk to be up and to arm."

Then he said "Good-night!" and with muffled oar
Silently rowed to the Charlestown shore,

Just as the moon rose over the bay,
Where swinging wide at her moorings lay
The *Somerset,* British man-of-war;
A phantom ship, with each mast and spar
Across the moon like a prison bar,
And a huge black hulk, that was magnified
By its own reflection in the tide.
Meanwhile, his friend through alley and street
Wanders and watches, with eager ears,
Till in the silence around him he hears
The muster of men at the barrack door,
The sound of arms, and the tramp of feet,
And the measured tread of the grenadiers,
Marching down to their boats on the shore.

Then he climbed the tower of the Old North
       Church,
By the wooden stairs, with stealthy tread,
To the belfry chamber overhead,
And startled the pigeons from their perch
On the sombre rafters, that round him made
Masses and moving shapes of shade,—
By the trembling ladder, steep and tall,
To the highest window in the wall,
Where he paused to listen and look down
A moment on the roofs of the town
And the moonlight flowing over all.

Beneath, in the churchyard, lay the dead,
In their night encampment on the hill,

Wrapped in silence so deep and still
That he could hear, like a sentinel's tread,
The watchful night-wind, as it went
Creeping along from tent to tent,
And seeming to whisper, "All is well!"
A moment only he feels the spell
Of the place and the hour, and the secret
      dread
Of the lonely belfry and the dead;
For suddenly all his thoughts are bent
On a shadowy something far away,
Where the river widens to meet the bay,—
A line of black that bends and floats
On the rising tide like a bridge of boats.

Meanwhile, impatient to mount and ride,
Booted and spurred, with a heavy stride
On the opposite shore walked Paul Revere.
Now he patted his horse's side,
Now he gazed at the landscape far and near,
Then, impetuous, stamped the earth,
And turned and tightened his saddle girth;
But mostly he watched with eager search
The belfry tower of the Old North Church,
As it rose above the graves on the hill,
Lonely and spectral and sombre and still.
And lo! as he looks, on the belfry's height
A glimmer, and then a gleam of light!
He springs to the saddle, the bridle he turns,

But lingers and gazes, till full on his sight
A second lamp in the belfry burns.

A hurry of hoofs in a village street,
A shape in the moonlight, a bulk in the dark,
And beneath, from the pebbles, in passing, a
  spark
Struck out by a steed flying fearless and fleet;
That was all! And yet, through the gloom and
  the light,
The fate of a nation was riding that night;
And the spark struck out by that steed, in his
  flight,
Kindled the land into flame with its heat.
He has left the village and mounted the steep,
And beneath him, tranquil and broad and
  deep,
Is the Mystic, meeting the ocean tides;
And under the alders that skirt its edge,
Now soft on the sand, now loud on the ledge,
Is heard the tramp of his steed as he rides.

It was twelve by the village clock
When he crossed the bridge into Medford
  town.
He heard the crowing of the cock,
And the barking of the farmer's dog,
And felt the damp of the river fog,
That rises after the sun goes down.

It was one by the village clock,
When he galloped into Lexington.
He saw the gilded weathercock
Swim in the moonlight as he passed,
And the meeting-house windows, black and
        bare,
Gaze at him with a spectral glare,
As if they already stood aghast
At the bloody work they would look upon.

It was two by the village clock,
When he came to the bridge in Concord town.
He heard the bleating of the flock,
And the twitter of birds among the trees,
And felt the breath of the morning breeze
Blowing over the meadow brown.
And one was safe and asleep in his bed
Who at the bridge would be first to fall,
Who that day would be lying dead,
Pierced by a British musket ball.

You know the rest. In the books you have read
How the British Regulars fired and fled,—
How the farmers gave them ball for ball,
From behind each fence and farmyard wall,
Chasing the redcoats down the lane,
Then crossing the fields to emerge again
Under the trees at the turn of the road,
And only pausing to fire and load.

So through the night rode Paul Revere;
And so through the night went his cry of alarm
To every Middlesex village and farm,—
A cry of defiance, and not of fear,
A voice in the darkness, a knock at the door,
And a word that shall echo for evermore!
For, borne on the night-wind of the Past,
Through all our history, to the last,
In the hour of darkness and peril and need,
The people will waken and listen to hear
The hurrying hoofbeats of that steed,
And the midnight message of Paul Revere.

# Barbara Frietchie

## JOHN GREENLEAF WHITTIER
### (1807–1892)

*Whittier was a Quaker and a prominent abolitionist. This stirring ballad is based on an actual incident of the Civil War.*

—✺—

Up from the meadows rich with corn,
Clear in the cool September morn,

The clustered spires of Frederick stand
Green-walled by the hills of Maryland.

Round about them orchards sweep,
Apple and peach tree fruited deep,

Fair as the garden of the Lord
To the eyes of the famished rebel horde,

On that pleasant morn of the early fall
When Lee marched over the mountain-wall;

Over the mountains winding down,
Horse and foot, into Frederick town.

Forty flags with their silver stars,
Forty flags with their crimson bars,

Flapped in the morning wind: the sun
Of noon looked down, and saw not one.

Up rose old Barbara Frietchie then,
Bowed with her fourscore years and ten;

Bravest of all in Frederick town,
She took up the flag the men hauled down;

In her attic window the staff she set,
To show that one heart was loyal yet.

Up the street came the Rebel tread,
Stonewall Jackson riding ahead.

Under his slouched hat left and right
He glanced; the old flag met his sight.

"Halt!"—the dust-brown ranks stood fast.
"Fire!"—out blazed the rifle-blast.

It shivered the window, pane and sash;
It rent the banner with seam and gash.

Quick, as it fell, from the broken staff
Dame Barbara snatched the silken scarf.

She leaned far out on the window-sill,
And shook it forth with a royal will.

"Shoot, if you must, this old gray head,
But spare your country's flag," she said.

A shade of sadness, a blush of shame,
Over the face of the leader came;

The nobler nature within him stirred
To life at that woman's deed and word;

"Who touches a hair of yon gray head
Dies like a dog! March on!" he said.

All day long through Frederick street
Sounded the tread of marching feet:

All day long that free flag tost
Over the heads of the Rebel host.

Ever its torn folds rose and fell
On the loyal winds that loved it well;

And through the hill-gaps sunset light
Shone over it with a warm good night.

Barbara Frietchie's work is o'er,
And the Rebel rides on his raids no more.

Honor to her! and let a tear
Fall, for her sake, on Stonewall's bier.

Over Barbara Frietchie's grave,
Flag of Freedom and Union, wave!

Peace and order and beauty draw
Round thy symbol of light and law;

And ever the stars above look down
On thy stars below in Frederick town!

# El Desdichado
## [The Disinherited]

GERARD DE NERVAL
(1808–1855)

*Nerval, an eccentric early surrealist, here creates a fantastic, dreamlike image of a wandering lover endlessly searching for what he has lost. The translation is by Robert Duncan.*

—⅏—

I am the dark one,—the widower,—the
      unconsoled,
The prince of Aquitaine at his stricken tower:
My sole *star* is dead,—and my constellated lute
Bears the black *sun* of the *Melancolia.*

In the night of the tomb, you who consoled me,
Give me back Mount Posilipo and the Italian sea,
The *flower* which pleased so my desolate heart,
And the trellis where the grape vine unites with
      the rose.

Am I Amor or Phoebus? . . . Lusignan or Biron?
My forehead is still red from the kiss of the
      queen;
I have dreamed in the grotto where the
      mermaid swims . . .

99

And two times victorious I have crosst the
 Acheron:
Modulating turn by turn on the lyre of Orpheus
The sighs of the saint and the cries of the fay.

# The Raven

## EDGAR ALLAN POE
## (1809–1849)

*Perhaps one of the most famous poems in American liter-
ature, "The Raven" tells a somber tale of lost love. Poe's
raven symbolizes misfortune and symbolically reinforces
the macabre tone of the work.*

—m—

Once upon a midnight dreary, while I
    pondered, weak and weary,
Over many a quaint and curious volume of
    forgotten lore,
While I nodded, nearly napping, suddenly
    there came a tapping,
As of someone gently rapping, rapping at my
    chamber door.
" 'Tis some visitor," I muttered, "tapping at my
    chamber door;
Only this, and nothing more."

Ah, distinctly I remember, it was in the bleak
    December,
And each separate dying ember wrought its
    ghost upon the floor.
Eagerly I wished the morrow; vainly I had
    sought to borrow

From my books surcease of sorrow, sorrow for
the lost Lenore,
For the rare and radiant maiden whom the
angels name Lenore,
Nameless here forevermore.

And the silken sad uncertain rustling of each
purple curtain
Thrilled me—filled me with fantastic terrors
never felt before;
So that now, to still the beating of my heart, I
stood repeating,
" 'Tis some visitor entreating entrance at my
chamber door,
Some late visitor entreating entrance at my
chamber door.
This is it, and nothing more."

Presently my soul grew stronger; hesitating
then no longer,
"Sir," said I, "or madam, truly your forgiveness
I implore;
But the fact is, I was napping, and so gently
you came rapping,
And so faintly you came tapping, tapping at
my chamber door,
That I scarce was sure I heard you." Here I
opened wide the door;—
Darkness there, and nothing more.

Deep into the darkness peering, long I stood there, wondering, fearing
Doubting, dreaming dreams no mortals ever dared to dream before;
But the silence was unbroken, and the stillness gave no token,
And the only word there spoken was the whispered word, "Lenore?"
This I whispered, and an echo murmured back the word, "Lenore!"
Merely this, and nothing more.

Back into the chamber turning, all my soul within me burning,
Soon again I heard a tapping, something louder than before,
"Surely," said I, "surely, that is something at my window lattice.
Let me see, then, what thereat is, and this mystery explore.
Let my heart be still a moment, and this mystery explore.
'Tis the wind, and nothing more."

Open here I flung the shutter, when, with many a flirt and flutter,
In there stepped a stately raven, of the saintly days of yore.
Not the least obeisance made he; not a minute stopped or stayed he;

But with mien of lord or lady, perched above
my chamber door.
Perched upon a bust of Pallas, just above my
chamber door,
Perched, and sat, and nothing more.

Then this ebony bird beguiling my sad fancy
into smiling,
By the grave and stern decorum of the
countenance it wore,
"Though thy crest be shorn and shaven thou,"
I said, "art sure no craven,
Ghastly, grim, and ancient raven, wandering
from the nightly shore.
Tell me what the lordly name is on the Night's
Plutonian shore."
Quoth the raven, "Nevermore."

Much I marveled this ungainly fowl to hear
discourse so plainly,
Though its answer little meaning, little
relevancy bore;
For we cannot help agreeing that no living
human being
Ever yet was blessed with seeing bird above
his chamber door,
Bird or beast upon the sculptured bust above
his chamber door,
With such name as "Nevermore."

But the raven, sitting lonely on that placid
      bust, spoke only
That one word, as if his soul in that one word
      he did outpour.
Nothing further then he uttered; not a feather
      then he fluttered;
Till I scarcely more than muttered, "Other
      friends have flown before;
On the morrow he will leave me, as my hopes
      have flown before."
Then the bird said, "Nevermore."

Startled at the stillness broken by reply so
      aptly spoken,
"Doubtless," said I, "what it utters is its only
      stock and store,
Caught from some unhappy master, whom
      unmerciful disaster
Followed fast and followed faster, till his songs
      one burden bore,—
Till the dirges of his hope that melancholy
      burden bore
Of 'Never—nevermore.'"

But the raven still beguiling all my fancy into
      smiling,
Straight I wheeled a cushioned seat in front of
      bird and bust and door;

Then, upon the velvet sinking, I betook myself
to linking
Fancy unto fancy, thinking what this ominous
bird of yore,
What this grim, ungainly, ghastly, gaunt, and
ominous bird of yore
Meant in croaking, "Nevermore."

Thus I sat engaged in guessing, but no
syllable expressing
To the fowl, whose fiery eyes now burned into
my bosom's core;
This and more I sat divining, with my head at
ease reclining
On the cushion's velvet lining that the
lamplight gloated o'er,
But whose velvet violet lining with the
lamplight gloating o'er
She shall press, ah, nevermore!

Then, methought, the air grew denser,
perfumed from an unseen censer
Swung by seraphim whose footfalls tinkled on
the tufted floor.
"Wretch," I cried, "thy God hath lent thee—by
these angels he hath sent thee
Respite—respite and nepenthe from thy
memories of Lenore!

Quaff, O quaff this kind nepenthe, and forget
    this lost Lenore!"
Quoth the raven, "Nevermore!"

"Prophet!" said I, "thing of evil!—prophet still,
    if bird or devil!
Whether tempter sent, or whether tempest
    tossed thee here ashore,
Desolate, yet all undaunted, on this desert
    land enchanted—
On this home by horror haunted—tell me truly,
    I implore:
Is there—is there balm in Gilead?—tell me—
    tell me I implore!"
Quoth the raven, "Nevermore."

"Prophet!" said I, "thing of evil—prophet still, if
    bird or devil!
By that heaven that bends above us—by that
    God we both adore—
Tell this soul with sorrow laden, if, within the
    distant Aidenn,
It shall clasp a sainted maiden, whom the
    angels name Lenore—
Clasp a rare and radiant maiden, whom the
    angels name Lenore?
Quoth the raven, "Nevermore."

"Be that word our sign of parting, bird or
       fiend!" I shrieked, upstarting—
"Get thee back into the tempest and the
       Night's Plutonian shore!
Leave no black plume as a token of that lie thy
       soul hath spoken!
Leave my loneliness unbroken!—quit the bust
       above my door!
Take thy beak from out my heart, and take thy
       form from off my door!"
Quoth the raven, "Nevermore."

And the raven, never flitting, still is sitting, still
       is sitting
On the pallid bust of Pallas just above my
       chamber door;
And his eyes have all the seeming of a
       demon's that is dreaming.
And the lamplight o'er him streaming throws
       the shadow on the floor;
And my soul from out that shadow that lies
       floating on the floor
Shall be lifted—nevermore!

# Ulysses

## ALFRED, LORD TENNYSON
## (1809–1892)

*A monologue by the central figure in Homer's Odyssey, this work exalts an indomitability that refuses to be limited by age and death.*

—⁓⁓—

It little profits that an idle king,
By this still hearth, among these barren crags,
Matched with an aged wife, I mete and dole
Unequal laws unto a savage race,
That hoard, and sleep, and feed, and know not
    me.
I cannot rest from travel; I will drink
Life to the lees. All times I have enjoyed
Greatly, have suffered greatly, both with those
That loved me, and alone; on shore, and when
Through scudding drifts the rainy Hyades
Vexed the dim sea. I am become a name;
For always roaming with a hungry heart
Much have I seen and known—cities of men
And manners, climates, councils, governments,
Myself not least, but honored of them all—
And drunk delight of battle with my peers,
Far on the ringing plains of windy Troy,
I am a part of all that I have met;

Yet all experience is an arch wherethrough
Gleams that untraveled world whose margin
    fades
Forever and forever when I move.
How dull it is to pause, to make an end,
To rust unburnished, not to shine in use!
As though to breathe were life! Life piled on
    life
Were all too little, and of one to me
Little remains; but every hour is saved
From that eternal silence, something more,
A bringer of new things; and vile it were
For some three suns to store and hoard myself,
And this gray spirit yearning in desire
To follow knowledge like a sinking star,
Beyond the utmost bound of human thought.

This is my son, mine own Telemachus,
To whom I leave the scepter and the isle—
Well-loved of me, discerning to fulfill
This labor, by slow prudence to make mild
A rugged people, and through soft degrees
Subdue them to the useful and the good.
Most blameless is he, centered in the sphere
Of common duties, decent not to fail
In offices of tenderness, and pay
Meet adoration to my household gods,
When I am gone. He works his work, I mine.

There lies the port; the vessel puffs her sail;
There gloom the dark, broad seas. My
     mariners,
Souls that have toiled, and wrought, and
     thought with me—
That ever with a frolic welcome took
The thunder and the sunshine, and opposed
Free hearts, free foreheads—you and I are old;
Old age hath yet his honor and his toil.
Death closes all; but something ere the end,
Some work of noble note, may yet be done,
Not unbecoming men that strove with gods.
The lights begin to twinkle from the rocks;
The long day wanes; the slow moon climbs;
     the deep
Moans round with many voices. Come, my
     friends,
'Tis not too late to seek a newer world.
Push off, and sitting well in order smite
The sounding furrows; for my purpose holds
To sail beyond the sunset, and the baths
Of all the western stars, until I die.
It may be that the gulfs will wash us down;
It may be we shall touch the Happy Isles,
And see the great Achilles, whom we knew.
Though much is taken, much abides; and
     though
We are not now that strength which in old
     days

Moved earth and heaven, that which we are,
     we are—
One equal temper of heroic hearts,
Made weak by time and fate, but strong in will
To strive, to seek, to find, and not to yield.

# Old Ironsides

## OLIVER WENDELL HOLMES
## (1809–1894)

*Outraged at the Navy's plan to destroy America's oldest frigate, the U.S.S.* Constitution, *in 1830, twenty-one-year-old Oliver Wendell Holmes mobilized a public outcry with this stirring verse. Old Ironsides now rests in Boston Harbor, the oldest commissioned ship in the United States Navy.*

—m—

Ay, tear her tattered ensign down!
Long has it waved on high,
And many an eye has danced to see
That banner in the sky;
Beneath it rung the battle shout,
And burst the cannon's roar;
The meteor of the ocean air
Shall sweep the clouds no more.

Her deck, once red with heroes' blood,
Where knelt the vanquished foe,
When winds were hurrying o'er the flood,
And waves were white below,
No more shall feel the victor's tread,
Or know the conquered knee;

The harpies of the shore shall pluck
The eagle of the sea!

Oh, better that her shattered bulk
Should sink beneath the wave;
Her thunders shook the mighty deep,
And there should be her grave;
Nail to the mast her holy flag,
Set every threadbare sail,
And give her to the god of storms,
The lightning and the gale!

# The Owl and the Pussycat

EDWARD LEAR
(1812–1888)

*Illustrator and writer Edward Lear, like Lewis Carroll, wrote much of his poetry in Nonsense Verse. In 1845 he authored for his patron's grandchildren* A Book of Nonsense, *which featured this poem.*

—m—

The Owl and the Pussycat went to sea
　　In a beautiful pea-green boat,
They took some honey, and plenty of money,
　　Wrapped up in a five-pound note.
The Owl looked up to the stars above,
　　And sang to a small guitar,
"O lovely Pussy! O Pussy my love,
　　What a beautiful Pussy you are,
　　　　You are,
　　　　You are!
What a beautiful Pussy you are!"

Pussy said to the Owl, "You elegant fowl!
　　How charmingly sweet you sing!
O let us be married! too long we have tarried:
　　But what shall we do for a ring?"
They sailed away, for a year and a day,
　　To the land where the Bong-tree grows

And there in a wood a Piggy-wig stood
   With a ring at the end of his nose,
      His nose,
      His nose,
With a ring at the end of his nose.

"Dear pig, are you willing to sell for one shilling
   Your ring?" Said the Piggy, "I will."
So they took it away, and were married next day
   By the Turkey who lives on the hill.
They dined on mince, and slices of quince,
   Which they ate with a runcible spoon;
And hand in hand, on the edge of the sand,
   They danced by the light of the moon,
      The moon,
      The moon,
They danced by the light of the moon.

# Memorabilia

## ROBERT BROWNING
## (1812–1889)

*Browning's great form was ironic dramatic monologue, and this brief, jewel-like example offers the quintessence of his art.*

Ah, did you once see Shelley plain,
   And did he stop and speak to you
And did you speak to him again?
   How strange it seems and new!

But you were living before that,
   And also you are living after;
And the memory I started at—
   My starting moves your laughter.

I crossed a moor, with a name of its own
   And a certain use in the world no doubt,
Yet a hand's-breadth of it shines alone
   'Mid the blank miles round about:

For there I picked up on the heather
   And there I put inside my breast
A molted feather, an eagle feather!
   Well, I forget the rest.

# Often Rebuked, Yet Always Back Returning

## EMILY BRONTË
## (1818–1848)

*Emily Brontë, one of the three Brontë sisters who initially published as men under the surname Bell, is best known for her only novel,* Wuthering Heights.

—ɯ—

Often rebuked, yet always back returning
    To those first feelings that were born with me,
And leaving busy chase of wealth and learning
    For idle dreams of things which cannot be:

Today, I will seek not the shadowy region;
    Its unsustaining vastness waxes drear,
And visions rising, legion after legion,
    Bring the unreal world too strangely near.

I'll walk but not in old heroic traces,
    And not in paths of high morality,
And not among the half-distinguished faces,
    The clouded forms of long-past history.

I'll walk where my own nature would be leading—
    It vexes me to choose another guide—
Where the gray flocks in ferny glens are feeding,
    Where the wild wind blows on the
        mountainside.

What have those lonely mountains worth
    revealing?
  More glory and more grief than I can tell:
The earth that wakes one human heart to
    feeling
  Can center both the worlds of Heaven and
    Hell.

# From Song of Myself

## WALT WHITMAN
## (1819–1892)

*One of the most influential poets in American literature, Walt Whitman, in his 1855 volume of poetry titled* Leaves of Grass, *sought to examine his own life as well as the national experience.*

A child said *What is the grass?* fetching it to
    me with full hands;
How could I answer the child? I do not know
    what it is any more than he.

I guess it must be the flag of my disposition,
    out of hopeful green stuff woven.

Or I guess it is the handkerchief of the Lord,
A scented gift and remembrancer designedly
    dropt,
Bearing the owner's name someway in the
    corners, that we may see and remark,
    and say *Whose?*

Or I guess the grass is itself a child, the
    produced babe of the vegetation.

Or I guess it is a uniform hieroglyphic,
And it means, Sprouting alike in broad zones
and narrow zones,
Growing among black folks as among white,
Kanuck, Tuckahoe, Congressman, Cuff, I give
them the same, I receive them the same.

And now it seems to me the beautiful uncut
hair of graves.

Tenderly will I use you curling grass,
It may be you transpire from the breasts of
young men,
It may be if I had known them I would have
loved them,
It may be you are from old people, or from
offspring taken soon out of their
mothers' laps,
And here you are the mothers' laps.

This grass is very dark to be from the white
heads of old mothers,
Darker than the colorless beards of old men,
Dark to come from under the faint red roofs of
mouths.

O I perceive after all so many uttering tongues,
And I perceive they do not come from the
roofs of mouths for nothing.

I wish I could translate the hints about the
dead young men and women,
And the hints about old men and mothers,
and the offspring taken soon out of their
laps.

What do you think has become of the young
and old men?
And what do you think has become of the
women and children?

They are alive and well somewhere,
The smallest sprout shows there is really no
death,
And if ever there was it led forward life, and
does not wait at the end to arrest it,
And ceas'd the moment life appeared.

All goes onward and outward, nothing
collapses,
And to die is different from what any one
supposed, and luckier.

# Battle Hymn of the Republic

## JULIA WARD HOWE
## (1819–1910)

*Howe was a fervent abolitionist, and her blend of religion and patriotism inspired Union troops during the American Civil War.*

—ɱ—

Mine eyes have seen the glory of the coming
    of the Lord,
He is trampling out the vintage where the
    grapes of wrath are stored,
He hath loosed the fateful lightning of His
    terrible swift sword,
His Truth is marching on.

Glory, glory hallelujah!
Glory, glory hallelujah!
Glory, glory hallelujah!
His truth is marching on.

I have seen Him in the watch fires of a
    hundred circling camps,
They have builded Him an altar in the evening
    dews and damps.
I can read His righteous sentence by the dim
    and flaring lamps,
His Day is marching on.

I have read His fiery gospel writ in burnished
rows of steel:
"As ye deal with My condemners, so with you
My grace shall deal."
Let the hero, born of woman, crush the
serpent with His heel,
As God is marching on.

He has sounded forth the trumpet that shall
never call retreat.
He is sifting out the hearts of men before His
judgment seat.
Oh! Be swift, my soul, to answer him, be
jubilant my feet,
Our God is marching on.

In the beauty of the lilies, Christ was born
across the sea,
With a glory in his bosom that transfigures you
and me.
As He died to make men holy, let us die to make
men free!
While God is marching on.

# Invitation to the Voyage

CHARLES BAUDELAIRE
(1821–1867)

*Baudelaire is most famous for his revolutionary work* Les Fleurs du Mal *(Flowers of Evil). In his writing, with its ornate, often shocking imagery, may be seen the future of modern verse up to the present day.*

—ɯ—

How sweet, my own,
Could we live alone
Over beyond the sea!
To love and to die
Indolently
In the land that's akin to thee!
Where the suns which rise
In the watery skies
Weave soft spells over my sight,
As thy false eyes do
When they flicker through
Their tears with a dim, strange light.

There all is beauty and symmetry,
Pleasure and calm and luxury.

Years that have gone
Have polished and shone

The things that would fill our room;
The flowers most rare
Which scent the air
In the richly ceiling'd gloom,
And the mirrors profound,
And the walls around
With Orient splendor hung,
To the soul would speak
Of things she doth seek
In her gentle native tongue.

There all is beauty and symmetry,
Pleasure and calm and luxury.

The canals are deep
Where the strange ships sleep
Far from the land of their birth;
To quench the fire
Of thy least desire
They have come from the ends of the earth.
The sunsets drown
Peaceful town
And meadow, and stagnant stream
In bistre and gold
And the world enfold
In a warm and luminous dream.

There all is beauty and symmetry,
Pleasure and calm and luxury.

# Dover Beach

## MATTHEW ARNOLD
## (1822—1888)

*A major English poet and social critic, Matthew Arnold here deplores the soullessness of the Victorian era, as well as its philistinism and materialism.*

—ᴍ—

The sea is calm tonight.
The tide is full, the moon lies fair
Upon the straits;—on the French coast the light
Gleams and is gone; the cliffs of England stand,
Glimmering and vast, out in the tranquil bay.
Come to the window, sweet is the night-air!
Only, from the long line of spray
Where the sea meets the moon-blanch'd land,
Listen! you hear the grating roar
Of pebbles which the waves draw back, and
      fling,
At their return, up the high strand,
Begin, and cease, and then again begin,
With tremulous cadence slow, and bring
The eternal note of sadness in.

Sophocles long ago
Heard it on the Aegean, and it brought
Into his mind the turbid ebb and flow

Of human misery; we
Find also in the sound a thought,
Hearing it by this distant northern sea.

The Sea of Faith
Was once, too, at the full, and round earth's
        shore
Lay like the folds of a bright girdle furl'd.
But now I only hear
Its melancholy, long, withdrawing roar,
Retreating, to the breath
Of the night-wind, down the vast edges drear
And naked shingles of the world.

Ah, love, let us be true
To one another! for the world, which seems
To lie before us like a land of dreams,
So various, so beautiful, so new,
Hath really neither joy, nor love, nor light,
Nor certitude, nor peace, nor help for pain;
And we are here as on a darkling plain
Swept with confused alarms of struggle and
        flight,
Where ignorant armies clash by night.

# Because I Could Not Stop for Death

## EMILY DICKINSON
## (1830–1886)

*Emily Dickinson is known mostly for poems that explore human consciousness, and her vision of immortality is the subject of her most memorable poem.*

—∽—

Because I could not stop for Death—
He kindly stopped for me—
The Carriage held but just Ourselves—
And Immortality.

We slowly drove—He knew no haste
And I had put away
My labor and my leisure too,
For His Civility—

We passed the School, where Children strove
At Recess—in the Ring—
We passed the Fields of Gazing Grain—
We passed the Setting Sun—

Or rather—He passed Us—
The Dews drew quivering and chill—
For only Gossamer, my Gown—
My Tippet—only Tulle—

We paused before a House that seemed
A Swelling of the Ground—
The Roof was scarcely visible—
The Cornice—in the Ground—

Since then—'tis Centuries—and yet
Feels shorter than the Day
I first surmised the Horses' Heads
Were toward Eternity.

# The Jabberwocky

LEWIS CARROLL
(1832–1898)

*Originally featured in Lewis Carroll's* Through the Looking Glass, *"The Jabberwocky" is written in Nonsense Verse, a literary technique of which Carroll was a master.*

—∞—

'Twas brillig, and the slithy toves
    Did gyre and gimble in the wabe;
All mimsy were the borogoves,
    And the mome raths outgrabe.

"Beware the Jabberwock, my son!
    The jaws that bite, the claws that catch!
Beware the Jubjub bird, and shun
    The frumious Bandersnatch!"

He took his vorpal sword in hand:
    Long time the manxome foe he sought—
So rested he by the Tumtum tree,
    And stood awhile in thought.

And as in uffish thought he stood,
    The Jabberwock, with eyes of flame,
Came whiffling through the tulgey wood,
    And burbled as it came!

One, two! One, two! And through and through
    The vorpal blade went snicker-snack!
He left it dead, and with its head
    He went galumphing back.

"And hast thou slain the Jabberwock?
    Come to my arms, my beamish boy!
O frabjous day! Callooh! Callay!"
    He chortled in his joy.

'Twas brillig, and the slithy toves
    Did gyre and gimble in the wabe;
All mimsy were the borogoves,
    And the mome raths outgrabe.

# Convergence of the Twain

## THOMAS HARDY
## (1840–1928)

*Hardy here ignores the popular tendency to romanticize the tragedy of the 1912 sinking of the* Titanic *in this cool, philosophical portrayal of its fated encounter with the iceberg.*

In a solitude of the sea
Deep from human vanity,
And the Pride of Life that planned her, stilly
couches she.

Steel chambers, late the pyres
Of her salamandrine fires,
Cold currents thrid, and turn to rhythmic tidal
lyres.

Over the mirrors meant
To glass the opulent
The sea-worm crawls—grotesque, slimed,
dumb, indifferent.

Jewels in joy designed
To ravish the sensuous mind
Lie lightless, all their sparkles bleared and
black and blind.

Dim moon-eyed fishes near
Gaze at the gilded gear
And query: "What does this vaingloriousness
down here?"

Well: while was fashioning
This creature of cleaving wing,
The Immanent Will that stirs and urges
everything

Prepared a sinister mate
For her—so gaily great—
A Shape of Ice, for the time far and dissociate.

And as the smart ship grew
In stature, grace, and hue,
In shadowy silent distance grew the Iceberg
too.

Alien they seemed to be:
No mortal eye could see
The intimate welding of their later history,

Or sign that they were bent
By paths coincident
On being anon twin halves of one august
event,

134

Till the Spinner of the Years
Said "Now!" And each one hears,
And consummation comes, and jars two
hemispheres.

# Spring and Fall
## [Margaret, Are You Grieving?]

### GERARD MANLEY HOPKINS
### (1844–1889)

*In this touching account of a young girl realizing the fragility of human life, a Victorian religious seriousness is given new vitality by the poet's distinctive modern metric and rhyme forms.*

———m———

Margaret, are you grieving
Over Goldengrove unleaving?
Leaves, like the things of man, you
With your fresh thoughts care for, can you?
Ah! as the heart grows older
It will come to such sights colder
By and by, nor spare a sigh
Though worlds of wanwood leafmeal lie;
And yet you will weep and know why.
Now no matter, child, the name:
Sorrow's springs are the same.
Nor mouth had, no nor mind, expressed
What heart heard of, ghost guessed:
It is the blight man was born for,
It is Margaret you mourn for.

# Tears Fall in My Heart

## PAUL VERLAINE
## (1844–1896)

*French poet Paul Verlaine had a passionate temperament, spending two years in prison for shooting his lover, Arthur Rimbaud.*

Tears fall in my heart
as rain falls on the town;
what is this numb hurt
that enters my heart?

Ah, the soft sound of rain
on roofs, on the ground!
To a dulled heart there came,
ah, the song of the rain!

Tears without reason
in the disheartened heart.
What? no trace of treason?
This grief's without reason.

It's far the worst pain
to never know why
without love or disdain
my heart has such pain!

# The New Colossus

## EMMA LAZARUS
## (1849–1887)

*Emma Lazarus's verse, inspired by the Statue of Liberty, marks a period in American history during which many Europeans immigrated to the United States. The juxtaposition of the image of America's "new colossus" with the one of Greek antiquity represents the two worlds the immigrants bridged.*

—⟋⟋⟋—

Not like the brazen giant of Greek fame,
With conquering limbs astride from land to land;
Here at our sea-washed, sunset gates shall stand
A mighty woman with a torch, whose flame
Is the imprisoned lightning, and her name
Mother of Exiles. From her beacon-hand
Glows worldwide welcome; her mild eyes command
The air-bridged harbor that twin cities frame.
"Keep ancient lands, your storied pomp!" cries she
With silent lips. "Give me your tired, your poor,
Your huddled masses yearning to breathe free,
The wretched refuse of your teeming shore.
Send these, the homeless, tempest-tost to me,
I lift my lamp beside the golden door!"

# Requiem

## Robert Louis Stevenson
### (1850–1894)

*In this poem Stevenson blurs the line between narrator and poet. "Requiem" was used as the epitaph on Stevenson's own tomb.*

Under the wide and starry sky
Dig the grave and let me lie:
Glad did I live and gladly die,
    And I laid me down with a will.

This be the verse you grave for me:
*Here he lies where he long'd to be;*
Home is the sailor, home from sea,
    And the hunter home from the hill.

# The Drunken Boat

### ARTHUR RIMBAUD
### (1854–1891)

*French Symbolist poet Arthur Rimbaud relied on the sensual powers of language to write evocative dreamlike poems, of which this is the best known.*

—◆—

I felt my guides no longer carried me—
as we sailed down the virgin Amazon,
the redskins nailed them to their painted stakes
naked, as targets for their archery.

I carried Flemish wheat or Swedish wood,
but had forgotten my unruly crew;
their conversation ended with their lives,
the river let me wander where I would.

Surf punished me, and threw my cargo out;
last winter I was breaking up on land.
I fled. These floating river villages
had never heard a more triumphant shout.

The green ooze spurting through my centerboard
was sweeter than sour apples to a boy—
it washed away the stains of puke and rotgut,
anchor and wheel were carried overboard.

The typhoon spun my silly needle round;
ten nights I scudded from the freighters' lights;
lighter than cork, I danced upon the surge
man calls the rolling coffin of his drowned.

Then heaven opened for the voyager.
I stared at archipelagoes of stars.
Was it on those dead watches that I died—
a million golden birds, Oh future Vigor!

I cannot watch these purple suns go down
like actors on the Aeschylean stage.
I'm drunk on water. I cry out too much—
Oh that my keel might break, and I might drown!

Shrunken and black against a twilight sky,
our Europe has no water. Only a pond
the cows have left, and a boy wades to launch
his paper boat frail as a butterfly.

Bathed in your languors, Waves, I have no wings
to cut across the wakes of cotton ships,
or fly against the flags of merchant kings,
or swim beneath the guns of prison ships.

# The Ballad of Reading Gaol

OSCAR WILDE
(1854–1900)

*Named for the English prison in which Wilde was incarcerated for his homosexual affair with Lord Alfred Douglas, "The Ballad of Reading Gaol," rich with biblical metaphor, is an exploration of betrayal and the poet's own sense of martyrdom.*

He did not wear his scarlet coat,
For blood and wine are red,
And blood and wine were on his hands
When they found him with the dead,
The poor dead woman whom he loved,
And murdered in her bed.

He walked amongst the Trial Men
In a suit of shabby gray;
A cricket cap was on his head,
And his step seemed light and gay;
But I never saw a man who looked
So wistfully at the day.

I never saw a man who looked
With such a wistful eye
Upon that little tent of blue

Which prisoners call the sky,
And at every drifting cloud that went
With sails of silver by.

I walked, with other souls in pain,
Within another ring,
And was wondering if the man had done
A great or little thing,
When a voice behind me whispered low,
*"That fellow's got to swing."*

Dear Christ! the very prison walls
Suddenly seemed to reel,
And the sky above my head became
Like a casque of scorching steel;
And, though I was a soul in pain,
My pain I could not feel.

I only knew what haunted thought
Quickened his step, and why
He looked upon the garish day
With such a wistful eye;
The man had killed the thing he loved,
And so he had to die.

Yet each man kills the thing he loves,
By each let this be heard,
Some do it with a bitter look,

Some with a flattering word,
The coward does it with a kiss,
The brave man with a sword!

Some kill their love when they are young,
And some when they are old;
Some strangle with the hands of Lust,
Some with the hands of Gold:
The kindest use a knife, because
The dead so soon grow cold.

Some love too little, some too long,
Some sell, and others buy;
Some do the deed with many tears,
And some without a sigh:
For each man kills the thing he loves,
Yet each man does not die.

He does not die a death of shame
On a day of dark disgrace,
Nor have a noose about his neck,
Nor a cloth upon his face,
Nor drop feet foremost through the floor
Into an empty space.

He does not sit with silent men
Who watch him night and day;
Who watch him when he tries to weep,

And when he tries to pray;
Who watch him lest himself should rob
The prison of its prey.

He does not wake at dawn to see
Dread figures throng his room,
The shivering Chaplain robed in white,
The Sheriff stern with gloom,
And the Governor all in shiny black,
With the yellow face of Doom.

He does not rise in piteous haste
To put on convict-clothes,
While some coarse-mouthed Doctor gloats,
and notes
Each new and nerve-twitched pose,
Fingering a watch whose little ticks
Are like horrible hammer-blows.

He does not feel that sickening thirst
That sands one's throat, before
The hangman with his gardener's gloves
Comes through the padded door,
And binds one with three leathern thongs,
That the throat may thirst no more.

He does not bend his head to hear
The Burial Office read,

Nor, while the anguish of his soul
Tells him he is not dead,
Cross his own coffin, as he moves
Into the hideous shed.

He does not stare upon the air
Through a little roof of glass:
He does not pray with lips of clay
For his agony to pass;
Nor feel upon his shuddering cheek
The kiss of Caiaphas.

# When I Was One-and-Twenty

## A. E. HOUSMAN
## (1859–1936)

*This poem incorporates one of Housman's favorite themes,*
*that of a naive youth learning of the world's cruelty.*

—⁂—

When I was one-and-twenty
   I heard a wise man say,
"Give crowns and pounds and guineas
   But not your heart away;
Give pearls away and rubies
   But keep your fancy free."
But I was one-and-twenty,
   No use to talk to me.

When I was one-and-twenty
   I heard him say again,
"The heart out of the bosom
   Was never given in vain;
'Tis paid with sighs a plenty
   And sold for endless rue."
And I am two-and-twenty
   And oh, 'tis true, 'tis true.

# The Gardener

## RABINDRANATH TAGORE
(1861–1941)

*Tagore's poetry, originally written in Bengali, is quite lyrical in its highly metaphorical and almost reverent explorations of love. (The poet was also renowned as a writer of songs.)*

—m—

Your questioning eyes are sad. They seek to know my meaning as the moon would fathom the sea.

I have bared my life before your eyes from end to end, with nothing hidden or held back. That is why you know me not.

If it were only a gem, I could break it into a hundred pieces and string them into a chain to put on your neck.

If it were only a flower, round and small and sweet, I could pluck it from its stem to set it in your hair.

But it is a heart, my beloved. Where are its shores and its bottom?

You know not the limits of this kingdom, still you are its queen.

If it were only a moment of pleasure it would flower in an easy smile, and you could see it and read it in a moment.

If it were merely a pain it would melt in limpid tears, reflecting its inmost secret without a word.
But it is love, my beloved.
Its pleasure and pain are boundless, and endless its wants and wealth.
It is as near to you as your life, but you can never wholly know it.

# Waiting for the Barbarians

## CONSTANTINE P. CAVAFY
## (1863–1933)

*This is a perfect example of how the Greek poet Cavafy's unique voice, characterized by a blend of literary and vernacular language, speaks frankly to readers, often expressing themes of political irony.*

—m—

What are we waiting for: packed in the forum?

    The barbarians are due here today.

Why isn't anything going on in the senate?
Why have the senators given up legislating?

    Because the barbarians are coming today.
    What's the point of senators and their laws
        now?
    When the barbarians get here, they'll do the
        legislating.

Why did our emperor set out so early
to sit on his throne at the city's main gate,
in state, wearing the crown?

    Because the barbarians are coming today
    and the emperor's waiting to receive their
        leader.

He's even got a citation to give him,
loaded with titles and imposing names.

Why have our two consuls and praetors
        shown up today
wearing their embroidered, their scarlet togas?
Why have they put on bracelets with so many
        amethysts,
rings sparkling with all those emeralds?
Why are they carrying elegant canes
so beautifully worked in silver and gold?

    Because the barbarians are coming today
    and things like that dazzle barbarians.

And why don't our distinguished orators push
        forward as usual
to make their speeches, say what they have to
        say?

    Because the barbarians are coming today
    and they're bored by rhetoric and public
        speaking.

Why this sudden bewilderment, this confusion?
(How serious everyone looks.)
Why are the streets and squares rapidly
        emptying,
everyone going home so lost in thought?

Because it's night and the barbarians
        haven't come.
And some people just in from the border
        say
there are no barbarians any longer.

Now what's going to happen to us without
        them?
The barbarians were a kind of solution.

# Casey at the Bat

## ERNEST THAYER
### (1863–1940)

*This mock-heroic narrative supplied epic grandeur to the last inning of a semi-professional baseball game, and in so doing conferred immortality upon itself as the greatest sports poem ever written.*

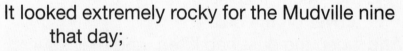

It looked extremely rocky for the Mudville nine
    that day;
The score stood two to four, with but an inning
    left to play.
So, when Cooney died at second, and
    Burrows did the same,
A pallor wreathed the features of the patrons
    of the game.

A straggling few got up to go, leaving there the
    rest,
With the hope which springs eternal within the
    human breast.
For they thought: "If only Casey could get a
    whack at that,"
They'd put even money now, with Casey at the
    bat.

But Flynn preceded Casey, and likewise so did
Blake,
And the former was a pudd'n, and the latter
was a fake.
So on that stricken multitude a deathlike
silence sat;
For there seemed but little chance of Casey's
getting to the bat.

But Flynn let drive a "single," to the
wonderment of all.
And the much-despised Blakey "tore the
cover off the ball."
And when the dust had lifted, and they saw
what had occurred,
There was Blakey safe at second, and Flynn
a-huggin' third.

Then from the gladdened multitude went up a
joyous yell—
It rumbled in the mountaintops, it rattled in the
dell;
It struck upon the hillside and rebounded on
the flat;
For Casey, mighty Casey, was advancing to
the bat.

There was ease in Casey's manner as he
stepped into his place,

There was pride in Casey's bearing and a
  smile on Casey's face;
And when responding to the cheers he lightly
  doffed his hat,
No stranger in the crowd could doubt 'twas
  Casey at the bat.

Ten thousand eyes were on him as he rubbed
  his hands with dirt,
Five thousand tongues applauded when he
  wiped them on his shirt;
Then when the writhing pitcher ground the ball
  into his hip,
Defiance glanced in Casey's eye, a sneer
  curled Casey's lip.

And now the leather-covered sphere came
  hurtling through the air,
And Casey stood a-watching it in haughty
  grandeur there.
Close by the sturdy batsman the ball
  unheeded sped;
"That ain't my style," said Casey. "Strike one,"
  the umpire said.

From the benches, black with people, there
  went up a muffled roar,
Like the beating of the storm waves on the
  stern and distant shore.

"Kill him! Kill the umpire!" shouted someone
on the stand;
And it's likely they'd have killed him had not
Casey raised his hand.

With a smile of Christian charity great Casey's
visage shone;
He stilled the rising tumult, he made the game
go on;
He signaled to the pitcher, and once more the
spheroid flew;
But Casey still ignored it, and the umpire said,
"Strike two."

"Fraud!" cried the maddened thousands, and
the echo answered "Fraud!"
But one scornful look from Casey and the
audience was awed;
They saw his face grow stern and cold, they
saw his muscles strain,
And they knew that Casey wouldn't let the
ball go by again.

The sneer is gone from Casey's lips, his teeth
are clenched in hate,
He pounds with cruel vengeance his bat upon
the plate;
And now the pitcher holds the ball, and now
he lets it go,

And now the air is shattered by the force of
    Casey's blow.

Oh, somewhere in this favored land the sun is
    shining bright,
The band is playing somewhere, and
    somewhere hearts are light;
And somewhere men are laughing, and
    somewhere children shout,
But there is no joy in Mudville: Mighty Casey
    has struck out.

# Gunga Din

## RUDYARD KIPLING
## (1865–1936)

*Incorporating a somewhat romantic view of British imperialism, Kipling, in verse that almost booms with rhythmic energy, here tells the tale of Gunga Din, the brave water carrier.*

—ɯɯ—

You may talk o' gin and beer
When you're quartered safe out 'ere,
An' you're sent to penny-fights an' Aldershot it;
But when it comes to slaughter
You will do your work on water,
An' you'll lick the bloomin' boots of 'im that's
     got it.
Now in Injia's sunny clime,
Where I used to spend my time
A-servin' of 'Er Majesty the Queen,
Of all them blackfaced crew
The finest man I knew
Was our regimental bhisti, Gunga Din.
    He was "Din! Din! Din!
You limpin' lump o' brick-dust, Gunga Din!
    Hi! slippery *hitherao!*
    Water, get it! *Panee lao!*
You squidgy-nosed old idol, Gunga Din."

The uniform 'e wore
Was nothin' much before,
An' rather less than 'arf o' that be'ind,
For a piece o' twisty rag
An' a goatskin water-bag
Was all the field-equipment 'e could find.
When the sweatin' troop-train lay
In a sidin' through the day,
Where the 'eat would make your bloomin'
    eyebrows crawl,
We shouted "Harry By!"
Till our throats were bricky-dry,
Then we wopped 'im 'cause 'e couldn't serve
    us all.
    It was "Din! Din! Din!
You 'eathen, where the mischief 'ave you
    been?
    You put some *juldee* in it
    Or I'll *marrow* you this minute
If you don't fill up my helmet, Gunga Din!"

'E would dot an' carry one
Till the longest day was done;
An' 'e didn't seem to know the use o' fear.
If we charged or broke or cut,
You could bet your bloomin' nut,
'E'd be waitin' fifty paces right flank rear.
With 'is *mussick* on 'is back,
'E would skip with our attack,

159

An' watch us till the bugles made "Retire,"
An' for all 'is dirty 'ide
'E was white, clear white, inside
When 'e went to tend the wounded under fire!
    It was "Din! Din! Din!"
With the bullets kickin' dust-spots on the
      green.
    When the cartridges ran out,
    You could hear the front-files shout,
"Hi! ammunition-mules an' Gunga Din!"

I shan't forgit the night
When I dropped be'ind the fight
With a bullet where my belt-plate should 'a'
      been.
I was chokin' mad with thirst,
An' the man that spied me first
Was our good old grinnin', gruntin' Gunga Din.
'E lifted up my 'ead,
An' he plugged me where I bled,
An 'e guv me 'arf-a-pint o' water-green:
It was crawlin' and it stunk,
But of all the drinks I've drunk,
I'm gratefullest to one from Gunga Din.
    It was "Din! Din! Din!
'Ere's a beggar with a bullet through 'is spleen;
    'E's chawin' up the ground,
    An 'e's kickin' all around:
For Gawd's sake git the water, Gunga Din!"

'E carried me away
To where a *dooli* lay,
An' a bullet come an' drilled the beggar clean.
'E put me safe inside,
An' just before 'e died,
"I 'ope you liked your drink," sez Gunga Din.
So I'll meet 'im later on
At the place where 'e is gone—
Where it's always double drill and no canteen;
'E'll be squattin' on the coals
Givin' drink to poor damned souls,
An' I'll get a swig in hell from Gunga Din!
    Yes, Din! Din! Din!
You Lazarushian-leather Gunga Din!
    Though I've belted you and flayed you,
    By the livin' Gawd that made you,
You're a better man than I am, Gunga Din!

# Lake Isle of Innisfree

## WILLIAM BUTLER YEATS
### (1865–1939)

*"Lake Isle of Innisfree" expresses the poet's yearning for the pastoral Ireland of myth and folklore, which was disappearing in the face of the modern world.*

—ᗰᗰ—

I will arise and go now, and go to Innisfree,
And a small cabin build there, of clay and
      wattles made:
Nine bean-rows will I have there, a hive for
      the honeybee,
And live alone in the bee-loud glade.

And I shall have some peace there, for
      peace comes dropping slow,
Dropping from the veils of the morning to
      where the cricket sings;
There midnight's all a glimmer, and noon a
      purple glow,
And evening full of the linnet's wings.

I will arise and go now, for always night and
      day

I hear lake water lapping with low sounds
        by the shore;
While I stand on the roadway, or on the
        pavements gray,
I hear it in the deep heart's core.

# Richard Cory

## EDWIN ARLINGTON ROBINSON
## (1869–1935)

*Set in a fictional New England village, this elegant little verse recounts an ironic, inexplicable tragedy.*

Whenever Richard Cory went down town,
We people on the pavement looked at him:
He was a gentleman from sole to crown,
Clean favored, and imperially slim.

And he was always quietly arrayed,
And he was always human when he talked;
But still he fluttered pulses when he said,
"Good morning," and he glittered when he
    walked.

And he was rich—yes, richer than a king—
And admirably schooled in every grace:
In fine, we thought that he was everything
To make us wish that we were in his place.

So on we worked, and waited for the light,
And went without the meat, and cursed the
    bread;
And Richard Cory, one calm summer night,
Went home and put a bullet through his head.

# We Wear the Mask

## PAUL LAWRENCE DUNBAR
## (1872–1906)

*A descendant of slaves, Paul Lawrence Dunbar triumphed over American racism and published four novels in addition to his short stories and poetry.*

—m—

We wear the mask that grins and lies,
It hides our cheeks and shades our eyes—
This debt we pay to human guile;
With torn and bleeding hearts we smile,
And mouth with myriad subtleties.

Why should the world be overwise,
In counting all our tears and sighs?
Nay, let them only see us, while
    We wear the mask.

We smile, but, O great Christ, our cries
To thee from tortured souls arise.
We sing, but oh the clay is vile
Beneath our feet, and long the mile;
But let the world dream otherwise,
    We wear the mask.

# The Cremation of Sam McGee

ROBERT SERVICE
(1874–1958)

*Famed as the poet of Yukon gold prospectors and north-
ern loggers, Service here recounts a straight-faced tall tale
in irresistibly cadenced verse.*

—〽—

*There are strange things done in the midnight
sun
By the men who moil for gold;
The Arctic trails have their secret tales
That would make your blood run cold;
The Northern Lights have seen queer sights,
But the queerest they ever did see
Was that night on the marge of Lake Lebarge
I cremated Sam McGee*

Now Sam McGee was from Tennessee,
where the cotton blooms and blows.
Why he left his home in the South to roam
'round the Pole, God only knows.
He was always cold but the land of gold
seemed to hold him like a spell;
Though he'd often say in his homely way
that he'd sooner live in Hell.

On a Christmas Day we were mushing our way
over the Dawson trail.
Talk of your cold! through the parka's fold
it stabbed like a driven nail.
If our eyes we'd close, then the lashes froze
till sometimes we couldn't see,
It wasn't much fun, but the only one
to whimper was Sam McGee.

And that very night, as we lay packed tight
in our robes beneath the snow,
And the dogs were fed, and the stars o'erhead
were dancing heel and toe,
He turned to me, and "Cap," says he,
"I'll cash in this trip, I guess;
And if I do, I'm asking that you
won't refuse my last request."

Well, he seemed so low that I couldn't say no;
then he says with a sort of moan,
"It's the cursed cold, and it's got right hold
till I'm chilled clean through to the bone.
Yet 'taint being dead—its my awful dread
of the icy grave that pains;
So I want you to swear that, foul or fair,
you'll cremate my last remains."

A pal's last need is a thing to heed,
so I swore I would not fail;

And we started on at the streak of dawn
but God! he looked ghastly pale.
He crouched on the sleigh, and he raved all day
of his home in Tennessee;
And before nightfall a corpse was all
that was left of Sam McGee.

There wasn't a breath in that land of death,
and I hurried, horror-driven,
With a corpse half hid that I couldn't get rid,
because of a promise given;
It was lashed to the sleigh, and it seemed to say,
"You may tax your brawn and brains,
But you promised true, and it's up to you
to cremate these last remains."

Now a promise made is a debt unpaid,
and the trail has its own stern code,
In the days to come, though my lips were dumb
in my heart how I cursed that load!
In the long, long night, by the lone firelight,
while the huskies, round in a ring,
Howled out their woes to the homeless
snows—
Oh God, how I loathed the thing!

And every day that quiet clay
seemed to heavy and heavier grow;

And on I went, though the dogs were spent
and the grub was getting low.
The trail was bad, and I felt half mad,
but I swore I would not give in;
And I'd often sing to the hateful thing,
and it hearkened with a grin.

Till I came to the marge of Lake Lebarge,
and a derelict there lay;
It was jammed in the ice, but I saw in a trice
it was called the *Alice May.*
And I looked at it, and I thought a bit,
and I looked at my frozen chum;
Then "Here," said I, with a sudden cry, "is my
cre-ma-tor-eum!"

Some planks I tore from the cabin floor
and I lit the boiler fire;
Some coal I found that was lying around,
and I heaped the fuel higher;
The flames just soared, and the furnace roared
such a blaze you seldom see,
And I burrowed a hole in the glowing coal,
and I stuffed in Sam McGee.

Then I made a hike, for I didn't like
to hear him sizzle so;
And the heavens scowled, and the huskies
howled,
and the wind began to blow.

It was icy cold, but the hot sweat rolled
down my cheeks, and I don't know why;
And the greasy smoke in an inky cloak
went streaking down the sky.

I do not know how long in the snow
I wrestled with grisly fear;
But the stars came out and they danced about
'ere again I ventured near;
I was sick with dread, but I bravely said,
"I'll just take a peep inside.
I guess he's cooked, and it's time I looked."
Then the door I opened wide.

And there sat Sam, looking cool and calm,
in the heart of the furnace roar;
And he wore a smile you could see a mile,
and he said, "Please close that door.
It's fine in here, but I greatly fear
you'll let in the cold and storm.
Since I left Plumtree, down in Tennessee,
it's the first time I've been warm."

*There are strange things done in the midnight
sun*
*By the men who moil for gold;*
*The Arctic trails have their secret tales*
*That would make your blood run cold;*

*The Northern Lights have seen queer sights,*
*But the queerest they ever did see*
*Was that night on the marge of Lake Lebarge*
*I cremated Sam McGee*

# Stopping by Woods on a Snowy Evening

## ROBERT FROST
## (1874–1963)

*Frost was once considered a regional poet, thematically focused on New England landscapes. A closer reading of Frost's work, however, especially this one, reveals a transcendent sense of the human condition.*

—⟋⟍—

Whose woods are these I think I know.
His house is in the village though;
He will not see me stopping here
To watch his woods fill up with snow.

My little horse must think it queer
To stop without a farmhouse near
Between the woods and frozen lake
The darkest evening of the year.

He gives his harness bells a shake
To ask if there is some mistake.
The only other sound's the sweep
Of easy wind and downy flake.

The woods are lovely, dark and deep.
But I have promises to keep,
And miles to go before I sleep,
And miles to go before I sleep.

# The Panther

## RAINER MARIA RILKE
## (1875–1926)

*In this poem Rilke describes a troubled peace, one born of
exile from the living world.*

—m—

So worn with passing through the bars,
His gaze holds nothing any more.
A thousand bars before him there might loom
And past the thousand bars no world.

The lissom stride of soundless padded pacing,
Revolving in the tiniest of rings,
Is like a dance of strength around a pivot,
Impaling in a trance a mighty will.

But rarely is the curtain of the eyeball
Softly parted. Then an image enters in
Which seeps through the tremulous stillness of
      the limbs
To reach the heart, where it expires.

# Sea Fever

## JOHN MASEFIELD
## (1878–1967)

*This poem, simple and direct in imagery and language, il-
lustrates Masefield's stylistic rebellion against Victorian lyrical and romantic conventions, while focusing on his love of
the sea, a theme that haunts most of his work.*

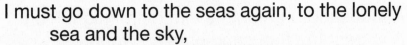

I must go down to the seas again, to the lonely
     sea and the sky,
And all I ask is a tall ship and a star to steer
     her by,
And the wheel's kick and the wind's song and
     the white sails shaking,
And a gray mist on the sea's face and a gray
     dawn breaking.

I must go down to the seas again, for the call
     of the running tide
Is a wild call and a clear call that may not be
     denied;
And all I ask is a windy day with the white
     clouds flying,
And the flung spray and the blown spume, and
     the sea gulls crying.

I must go down to the seas again, to the
vagrant gypsy life,
To the gull's way and the whale's way where
the wind's like a whetted knife;
And all I ask is a merry yarn from a laughing
fellow rover,
And quiet sleep and a sweet dream when the
long trick's over.

# Fog

## CARL SANDBURG
## (1878–1967)

*Also well known for his American folktales, Sandburg here
depicts a mysterious natural beauty in a few short lines.*

—◊◊◊—

The fog comes
on little cat feet.

It sits looking
over harbor and city
on silent haunches
and then moves on.

# General William Booth Enters into Heaven

## VACHEL LINDSAY
## (1879–1931)

*The poet's incantational voice comes alive in this poem that is a Salvation Army service, with brass band accompaniment and sung to the tune of "The Blood of the Lamb."*

———

[*Bass drum beaten loudly.*]

Booth led boldly with his big bass drum—
(Are you washed in the blood of the Lamb?)
The Saints smiled gravely and they said: "He's
      come."
(Are you washed in the blood of the Lamb?)
Walking lepers followed, rank on rank,
Lurching bravoes from the ditches dank,
Drabs from the alleyways and drug fiends pale—
Minds still passion-ridden, soul-powers frail:—
Vermin-eaten saints with mouldy breath,
Unwashed legions with the ways of Death—
(Are you washed in the blood of the Lamb?)

[*Banjos.*]

Every slum had sent its half-a-score
The round world over. (Booth had groaned for
      more.)

Every banner that the wide world flies
Bloomed with glory and transcendent dyes.
Big-voiced lasses made their banjos bang,
Tranced, fanatical they shrieked and sang:—
"Are you washed in the blood of the Lamb?"
Hallelujah! It was queer to see
Bull-necked convicts with that land make free.
Loons with trumpets blowed a blare, blare,
     blare
On, on upward thro' the golden air!
(Are you washed in the blood of the Lamb?)

[*Bass drum slower and softer.*]

Booth died blind and still by Faith he trod,
Eyes still dazzled by the ways of God.
Booth led boldly, and he looked the chief
Eagle countenance in sharp relief,
Beard a-flying, air of high command
Unabated in that holy land.

[*Sweet flute music.*]

Jesus came from out the court-house door,
Stretched his hands above the passing poor.
Booth saw not, but led his queer ones there
Round and round the mighty court-house
     square.
Then in an instant all that blear review

Marched on spotless, clad in raiment new.
The lame were straightened, withered limbs
      uncurled
And blind eyes opened on a new, sweet world.

[*Bass drum louder.*]

Drabs and vixens in a flash made whole!
Gone was the weasel-head, the snout, the
      jowl!
Sages and sibyls now, and athletes clean,
Rulers of empires, and of forests green!

[*Grand chorus of all instruments. Tambourines to
      the foreground.*]

The hosts were sandaled, and their wings
      were fire!
(Are you washed in the blood of the Lamb?)
But their noise played havoc with the angel-
      choir.
(Are you washed in the blood of the Lamb?)
O shout Salvation! It was good to see
Kings and Princes by the Lamb set free.
The banjos rattled and the tambourines
Jing-jing-jingled in the hands of Queens.

[*Reverently sung, no instruments.*]

179

And when Booth halted by the curb for prayer
He saw his Master thro' the flag-filled air.
Christ came gently with a robe and crown
For Booth the soldier, while the throng knelt
      down.
He saw King Jesus. They were face to face,
And he knelt a-weeping in that holy place.
Are you washed in the blood of the Lamb?

# Peter Quince at the Clavier

WALLACE STEVENS
(1879–1955)

*This poem exemplifies Stevens's desire to conceptualize the ineffable. Here he weaves narrative, imagery, and sound into a poetic vision of music that evokes repressed passion.*

## I

Just as my fingers on these keys
Make music, so the selfsame sounds
On my spirit make a music, too.

Music is feeling, then, not sound;
And thus it is that what I feel,
Here in this room, desiring you,

Thinking of your blue-shadowed silk,
Is music. It is like the strain
Waked in the elders by Susanna.

Of a green evening, clear and warm,
She bathed in her still garden, while
The red-eyed elders watching, felt

The basses of their beings throb
In witching chords, and their thin blood
Pulse pizzicati of Hosanna.

## II

In the green water, clear and warm,
Susanna lay.
She searched
The touch of springs,
And found
Concealed imaginings.
She sighed,
For so much melody.

Upon the bank, she stood
In the cool
Of spent emotions.
She felt, among the leaves,
The dew
Of old devotions.

She walked upon the grass,
Still quavering.
The winds were like her maids,
On timid feet,
Fetching her woven scarves,
Yet wavering.

A breath upon her hand
Muted the night.
She turned—
A cymbal crashed,
And roaring horns.

### III

Soon, with a noise like tamborines,
Came her attendant Byzantines.

They wondered why Susanna cried
Against the elders by her side;

And as they whispered, the refrain
Was like a willow swept by rain.

Anon, their lamps' uplifted flame
Revealed Susanna and her shame.

And then, the simpering Byzantines
Fled, with a noise like tamborines.

### IV

Beauty is momentary in the mind—
The fitful tracing of a portal;
But in the flesh it is immortal.

The body dies; the body's beauty lives.
So evenings die, in their green going,
A wave, interminably flowing.

So gardens die, their meek breath scenting
The cowl of winter, done repenting.
So maidens die, to the auroral
Celebration of a maiden's choral.

Susanna's music touched the bawdy strings
Of those white elders; but, escaping,
Left only Death's ironic scraping.
Now, in its immortality, it plays
On the clear viol of her memory,
And makes a constant sacrament of praise.

# The Highwayman

ALFRED NOYES
(1880–1958)

*Known for his stirring lyricism, Noyes recounts a vividly romantic tale in this dramatic modern ballad.*

—ɯ—

The wind was a torrent of darkness among the
     gusty trees,
The moon was a ghostly galleon tossed upon
     cloudy seas,
The road was a ribbon of moonlight over the
     purple moor,
And the highwayman came riding—
Riding—riding—
The highwayman came riding, up to the old
     inn-door.

He'd a French cocked-hat on his forehead, a
     bunch of lace at his chin,
A coat of the claret velvet, and breeches of
     brown doe-skin;
They fitted with never a wrinkle. His boots
     were up to the thigh.
And he rode with a jeweled twinkle,
His pistol butt a-twinkle,
His rapier hilt a-twinkle, under the jeweled sky.

Over the cobbles he clattered and clashed in
the dark inn-yard;
He tapped with his whip on the shutters, but
all was locked and barred;
He whistled a tune to the window, and who
should be waiting there
But the landlord's black-eyed daughter,
Bess, the landlord's daughter,
Plaiting a dark red love-knot into her long
black hair.

And dark in the dark old inn-yard a stable-
wicket creaked
Where Tim the ostler listened; his face was
white and peaked;
His eyes were hollows of madness, his hair
like moldy hay,
But he loved the landlord's daughter;
The landlord's red-lipped daughter;
Dumb as a dog he listened, and he heard the
robber say—
"One kiss, my bonny sweetheart, I'm after a
prize tonight,
But I shall be back with the yellow gold before
the morning light;
Yet, if they press me sharply, and harry me
through the day,
Then look for me by moonlight,
Watch for me by moonlight,

I'll come to thee by moonlight, though hell
    should bar the way."

He rose upright in the stirrups: He scarce
    could reach her hand,
But she loosened her hair i' the casement. Her
    face burnt like a brand
As the black cascade of perfume came
    tumbling over his breast;
And he kissed its waves in the moonlight,
(Oh, sweet, black waves in the moonlight!)
Then he tugged at his rein in the moonlight,
    and galloped away to the west.

He did not come in the dawning; he did not
    come at noon;
And out o' the tawny sunset, before the rise o'
    the moon,
When the road was a gypsy's ribbon, looping
    the purple moor,
A red-coat troop came marching—
Marching—marching—
King George's men came marching, up to the
    old inn-door.

They said no word to the landlord; they drank
    his ale instead;
But they gagged his daughter and bound her
    to the foot of her narrow bed.

Two of them knelt at her casement, with
	muskets at their side!
There was death at every window;
And hell at one dark window;
For Bess could see, through her casement,
	the road that he would ride.

They had tied her up to attention, with many a
	sniggering jest;
They had bound a musket beside her, with the
	muzzle beneath her breast!
"Now, keep good watch!" and they kissed her.
She heard the doomed man say—
Look for me by moonlight;
Watch for me by moonlight;
I'll come to thee by moonlight, though hell
	should bar the way!

She twisted her hands behind her; but all the
	knots held good!
She writhed her hands till her fingers were wet
	with sweat or blood!
They stretched and strained in the darkness,
	and the hours crawled by like years,
Till, now, on the stroke of midnight,
Cold, on the stroke of midnight,
The tip of one finger touched it! The trigger at
	least was hers!

The tip of one finger touched it; she strove no
    more for the rest!
Up, she stood up to attention, with the barrel
    beneath her breast,
She would not risk their hearing; she would
    not strive again;
For the road lay bare in the moonlight;
Blank and bare in the moonlight;
And the blood of her veins in the moonlight
    throbbed to her love's refrain.

Tlot-tlot! Tlot-tlot! Had they heard it? The
    horse-hoofs ringing clear;
Tlot-tlot, tlot-tlot, in the distance? Were they
    deaf that they did not hear?
Down the ribbon of moonlight, over the brow
    of the hill,
The highwayman came riding,
Riding, riding!
The red-coats looked to their priming! She
    stood up, straight and still!

Tlot-tlot, in the frosty silence! Tlot-tlot, in the
    echoing night!
Nearer he came and nearer! Her face was like
    a light!
Her eyes grew wide for a moment; she drew
    one last deep breath,
Then her finger moved in the moonlight,

Her musket shattered the moonlight;
Shattered her breast in the moonlight and
    warned him—with her death.

He turned; he spurred to the westward; he did
    not know who stood
Bowed, with her head o'er the musket,
    drenched with her own blood!
Not till the dawn he heard it, and his face grew
    gray to hear
How Bess, the landlord's daughter,
The landlord's black-eyed daughter,
Had watched for her love in the moonlight,
    and died in the darkness there.

Back, he spurred like a madman, shrieking a
    curse to the sky,
With the white road smoking behind him, and
    his rapier brandished high.
Blood-red were his spurs i' the golden noon;
    wine-red was his velvet coat;
When they shot him down on the highway,
Down like a dog on the highway,
And he lay in his blood on the highway, with
    the bunch of lace at his throat.

And still of a winter's night, they say, when the
    wind is in the trees,
When the moon is a ghostly galleon tossed
    upon cloudy seas,

When the road is a ribbon of moonlight over
        the purple moor,
A highwayman comes riding—
Riding—riding—
A highwayman comes riding, up to the old
        inn-door.

Over the cobbles he clatters and clangs in the
        dark inn-yard;
And he taps with his whip on the shutters, but
        all is locked and barred;
He whistles a tune to the window, and who
        should be waiting there
But the landlord's black-eyed daughter,
Bess, the landlord's daughter,
Plaiting a dark red love-knot into her long
        black hair.

# The Red Wheelbarrow

## WILLIAM CARLOS WILLIAMS
## (1883–1963)

*Williams was notable for writing about things, not ideas. This poem is a stunning example of how his simple, striking wording illuminates ordinary "things" in extraordinary light.*

so much depends
upon

a red wheel
barrow

glazed with rain
water

beside the white
chickens

# Ancient Music

## EZRA POUND
### (1885–1972)

*Pound believed that great literature should be simply charged with the utmost meaning. This poem almost demands to be declaimed in the most passionate voice possible.*

—ɱ—

Winter is icummen in,
Lhude sing Goddamm,
Raineth drop and staineth slop,
And how the wind doth ramm!
    Sing: Goddamm.
Skiddeth bus and sloppeth us,
An ague hath my ham.
Freezeth river, turneth liver,
    Damn you, sing: Goddamm.
Goddamm, Goddamm, 'tis why I am,
    Goddamm.
    So 'gainst the winter's balm.
Sing goddamm, damm, sing Goddamm,
Sing goddamm, sing goddamm, DAMM.

# The Love Song of J. Alfred Prufrock

## T. S. ELIOT
(1888–1965)

*The Italian epigraph quotes a damned soul that Dante encounters on his journey through Hell in the* Inferno. *He explains to Dante that he answers his questions only because he believes that Dante will never return to the living world (and therefore his words carry no consequences). The narrator of this poem, similarly, will not act on his desires for fear of rejection, creating, in a sense, his own hell on earth.*

—∞—

*S'io credesse che mia risposta fosse*
*A persona che mai tornasse al mondo,*
*Questa fiamma staria senza piu scosse.*
*Ma percioche giammai di questo fondo*
*Non torno vivo alcun, s'i'odo il vero,*
*Senza tema d'infamia ti rispondo.*

Let us go then, you and I,
When the evening is spread out against the
     sky
Like a patient etherized upon a table;
Let us go, through certain half-deserted
     streets,
The muttering retreats
Of restless nights in one-night cheap hotels

And sawdust restaurants with oyster-shells:
Streets that follow like a tedious argument
Of insidious intent
To lead you to an overwhelming question . . .
Oh, do not ask, "What is it?"
Let us go and make our visit.

In the room the women come and go
Talking of Michelangelo.

The yellow fog that rubs its back upon the
     window-panes,
The yellow smoke that rubs its muzzle on the
     window-panes,
Licked its tongue into the corners of the
     evening,
Lingered upon the pools that stand in drains,
Let fall upon its back the soot that falls from
     chimneys,
Slipped by the terrace, made a sudden leap,
And seeing that it was a soft October night,
Curled once about the house, and fell asleep.

And indeed there will be time
For the yellow smoke that slides along the
     street,
Rubbing its back upon the window-panes;
There will be time, there will be time
To prepare a face to meet the faces that you
     meet;

There will be time to murder and create,
And time for all the works and days of hands
That lift and drop a question on your plate;
Time for you and time for me,
And time yet for a hundred indecisions,
And for a hundred visions and revisions,
Before the taking of a toast and tea.

In the room the women come and go
Talking of Michelangelo.

And indeed there will be time
To wonder, "Do I dare?" and, "Do I dare?"
Time to turn back and descend the stair,
With a bald spot in the middle of my hair—
(They will say: "How his hair is growing thin!")
My morning coat, my collar mounting firmly to
      the chin,
My necktie rich and modest, but asserted by a
      simple pin—
(They will say: "But how his arms and legs are
      thin!")
Do I dare
Disturb the universe?
In a minute there is time
For decisions and revisions which a minute
      will reverse.

For I have known them all already, known
        them all:
Have known the evenings, mornings, afternoons,
I have measured out my life with coffee spoons;
I know the voices dying with a dying fall
Beneath the music from a farther room.
    So how should I presume?

And I have known the eyes already, known
        them all—
The eyes that fix you in a formulated phrase,
And when I am formulated, sprawling on a pin,
When I am pinned and wriggling on the wall,
Then how should I begin
To spit out all the butt-ends of my days and
        ways?
    And how should I presume?

And I have known the arms already, known
        them all—
Arms that are braceleted and white and bare
(But in the lamplight, downed with light brown
        hair!)
Is it perfume from a dress
That makes me so digress?
Arms that lie along a table, or wrap about a
        shawl.
    And should I then presume?
    And how should I begin?

Shall I say, I have gone at dusk through narrow
        streets
And watched the smoke that rises from the
        pipes
Of lonely shirt-sleeves, leaning out of
        windows? . . .

I should have been a pair of ragged claws
Scuttling across the floors of silent seas.

And the afternoon, the evening, sleeps so
        peacefully!
Smoothed by long fingers,
Asleep . . . tired . . . or it malingers,
Stretched on the floor, here beside you and
        me.
Should I, after tea and cakes and ices,
Have the strength to force the moment to its
        crisis?
But though I have wept and fasted, wept and
        prayed,
Though I have seen my head (grown slightly
        bald) brought in upon a platter,
I am no prophet—and here's no great matter;
I have seen the moment of my greatness
        flicker,
And I have seen the eternal Footman hold my
        coat, and snicker,
And in short, I was afraid.

And would it have been worth it, after all,
After the cups, the marmalade, the tea,
Among the porcelain, among some talk of you
      and me,
Would it have been worth while,
To have bitten off the matter with a smile,
To have squeezed the universe into a ball
To roll it towards some overwhelming question,
To say: "I am Lazarus, come from the dead,
Come back to tell you all, I shall tell you all"—
If one, settling a pillow by her head
    Should say: "That is not what I meant at all;
    That is not it, at all."

And would it have been worth it, after all,
Would it have been worth while,
After the sunsets and the dooryards and the
      sprinkled streets,
After the novels, after the teacups, after the
      skirts that trail along the floor—
And this, and so much more?—
It is impossible to say just what I mean!
But as if a magic lantern threw the nerves in
      patterns on a screen:
Would it have been worth while
If one, settling a pillow or throwing off a shawl,
And turning toward the window, should say:
    "That is not it at all,
    That is not what I meant, at all."

No! I am not Prince Hamlet, nor was meant to
    be;
Am an attendant lord, one that will do
To swell a progress, start a scene or two,
Advise the prince; no doubt, an easy tool,
Deferential, glad to be of use,
Politic, cautious, and meticulous;
Full of high sentence, but a bit obtuse;
At times, indeed, almost ridiculous—
Almost, at times, the Fool.

I grow old . . . I grow old . . .
I shall wear the bottoms of my trousers rolled.

Shall I part my hair behind? Do I dare to eat a
    peach?
I shall wear white flannel trousers, and walk
    upon the beach.
I have heard the mermaids singing, each to
    each.

I do not think that they will sing to me.

I have seen them riding seaward on the
    waves
Combing the white hair of the waves blown
    back
When the wind blows the water white and
    black.

We have lingered in the chambers of the sea
By sea-girls wreathed with seaweed red and
    brown
Till human voices wake us, and we drown.

# First Fig

## EDNA ST. VINCENT MILLAY
## (1892–1950)

*This poem embodies the spirit and energy of Millay, whose voice of rebellious youth typifies her work.*

My candle burns at both ends;
　It will not last the night;
But ah, my foes, and oh, my friends—
　It gives a lovely light!

# Dulce Et Decorum Est

WILFRED OWEN
(1893–1918)

*Considered one of the most important war poets of all time, Owen here expresses the horrors of war with intense imagery and irony. The Latin title is from a traditional saying: "It is sweet and proper to die for one's country."*

—⚍—

Bent double, like old beggars under sacks,
Knock-kneed, coughing like hags, we cursed
    through sludge,
Till on the haunting flares we turned our backs
And towards our distant rest began to trudge.
Men marched asleep. Many had lost their
    boots
But limped on, blood-shod. All went lame; all
    blind;
Drunk with fatigue; deaf even to the hoots
Of tired, outstripped Five-Nines that dropped
    behind.

Gas! Gas! Quick, boys!—An ecstasy of
    fumbling,
Fitting the clumsy helmets just in time;
But someone still was yelling out and
    stumbling,

And flound'ring like a man in fire or lime . . .
Dim, through the misty panes and thick green
    light,
As under a green sea, I saw him drowning.

In all my dreams, before my helpless sight,
He plunges at me, guttering, choking,
    drowning.

If in some smothering dreams you too could
    pace
Behind the wagon that we flung him in,
And watch the white eyes writhing in his face,
His hanging face, like a devil's sick of sin;
If you could hear, at every jolt, the blood
Come gargling from the froth-corrupted lungs,
Obscene as cancer, bitter as the cud
Of vile, incurable sores on innocent
    tongues,—
My friend, you would not tell with such high
    zest
To children ardent for some desperate glory,
The old Lie: *Dulce et decorum est
Pro patria mori.*

# Buffalo Bill's

## E. E. CUMMINGS
### (1894–1962)

*Cummings challenges our assumptions about poetic form in this ironic tribute to Buffalo Bill Cody by making the figure of Death a participant in Cody's Wild West Show.*

Buffalo Bill's
defunct
    who used to
    ride a watersmooth-silver
        stallion
and break onetwothreefourfive
    pigeonsjustlikethat
              Jesus
he was a handsome man
     and what i want to know is
how do you like your blueeyed boy
Mister Death

# From *Lament for Ignacio Sanchez Mejias*
## [Absence of the Soul 4]

FEDERICO GARCÍA LORCA
(1898–1936)

*Although he was born into a wealthy Spanish family, Lorca often focused on the plight of the local peasants. In vivid, symbolic language he painted dramatic, sensitive pictures of their dreams and realities.*

—ɯ—

The bull does not know you, nor the fig tree,
nor horses, nor the ants on your floors.
The child does not know you, nor the evening,
because your death is forever.

The saddleback of rock does not know you,
nor the black satin where you tore apart.
Your silent recollection does not know you
because your death is forever.

Autumn will return bringing snails,
misted-over grapes, and clustered mountains,
but none will wish to gaze in your eyes
because your death is forever.

Because your death is forever,
like everyone's who ever died on Earth,

like all dead bodies discarded
on rubbish heaps with mongrels' corpses.

No one knows you. No one. But I sing you—
sing your profile and your grace, for later on.
The signal ripeness of your mastery.
The way you sought death out, savored its taste.
The sadness just beneath your gay valor.

Not soon, if ever, will Andalusia see
so towering a man, so venturesome.
I sing his elegance with words that moan
and remember a sad breeze in the olive groves.

# Harlem
## [Dream Deferred]

### LANGSTON HUGHES
### (1902–1967)

*One of the leading writers of the Harlem Renaissance, Hughes here blends the rhythms of black oral tradition with undertones of jazz and blues to express his powerful message.*

—〰—

*What happens to a dream deferred?*

Does it dry up
like a raisin in the sun?
Or fester like a sore—
And then run?
Does it stink like rotten meat?
Or crust and sugar over
like a syrupy sweet?

Maybe it just sags
like a heavy load.

*Or does it explode?*

# Incident

COUNTEE CULLEN
(1903–1946)

*Although considered a poet of the Harlem Renaissance, Cullen, a contemporary of Langston Hughes, retained a more traditional lyrical style, which gives this particular poem a nursery-song quality despite its provocative subject matter.*

*(For Eric Walrond)*

Once riding in old Baltimore,
Heart-filled, head-filled with glee,
I saw a Baltimorean
Keep looking straight at me.

Now I was eight and very small,
And he was no whit bigger,
And so I smiled, but he poked out
His tongue, and called me, "Nigger."

I saw the whole of Baltimore
From May until December;
Of all the things that happened there
That's all that I remember.

# Poetry

## PABLO NERUDA
## (1904–1973)

*This poem, eloquently philosophizing Neruda's definition of poetry, was featured in the award-winning Italian film* Il Postino, *in which Pablo Neruda was a central character.*

—ɯ—

And it was at that age . . . Poetry arrived
in search of me. I don't know, I don't know
     where
it came from, from winter or a river.
I don't know how or when,
no, they were not voices, they were not
words, nor silence,
but from a street I was summoned,
from the branches of night,
abruptly from the others,
among violent fires
or returning alone,
there I was without a face
and it touched me.

I did not know what to say, my mouth
had no way
with names,

my eyes were blind,
and something started in my soul,
fever or forgotten wings,
and I made my own way,

deciphering
that fire,
and I wrote the first faint line,
faint, without substance, pure
nonsense,
pure wisdom
of someone who knows nothing,
and suddenly I saw
the heavens
unfastened
and open,
planets,
palpitating plantations,
shadow perforated,
riddled
with arrows, fire and flowers,
the winding night, the universe.

And I, infinitesimal being,
drunk with the great starry
void,
likeness, image of
mystery,

felt myself a pure part
of the abyss,
I wheeled with the stars,
my heart broke loose on the wind.

# Funeral Blues

## W. H. AUDEN
## (1907–1973)

*Few artists have approached Auden's "Funeral Blues" in expressing the grief of losing a lover. Many a viewer was moved to tears when the poem was read aloud in the funeral scene of the film* Four Weddings and a Funeral.

—m—

Stop all the clocks, cut off the telephone,
Prevent the dog from barking with a juicy
      bone,
Silence the pianos and with muffled drum
Bring out the coffin, let the mourners come.

Let aeroplanes circle moaning overhead
Scribbling on the sky the message He is Dead,
Put crepe bows round the white necks of the
      public doves,
Let the traffic policemen wear black cotton
      gloves.

He was my North, my South, my East and West,
My working week and my Sunday rest,
My noon, my midnight, my talk, my song;
I thought that love would last for ever: I was
      wrong.

The stars are not wanted now: put out every
      one;
Pack up the moon and dismantle the sun;
Pour away the ocean and sweep up the wood.
For nothing now can ever come to any good.

# Visits to St. Elizabeth's

## ELIZABETH BISHOP
### (1911–1979)

*This poem is based on an actual visit Bishop made to see the poet Ezra Pound when he was confined in a mental hospital. The precise attention to detail that is her trademark, and the poem's relentlessly accelerating rhythmic drive, set this poem apart.*

This is the house of Bedlam.

This is the man
that lies in the house of Bedlam.

This is the time
of the tragic man
that lies in the house of Bedlam.

This is a wristwatch
telling the time
of the talkative man
that lies in the house of Bedlam.

This is a sailor
wearing the watch
that tells the time

of the honored man
that lies in the house of Bedlam.

This is the roadstead all of board
reached by the sailor
wearing the watch
that tells the time
of the old, brave man
that lies in the house of Bedlam.

These are the years and the walls of the ward,
the winds and clouds of the sea of board
sailed by the sailor
wearing the watch
that tells the time
of the cranky man
that lies in the house of Bedlam.

This is a Jew in a newspaper hat
that dances weeping down the ward
over the creaking sea of board
beyond the sailor
winding his watch
that tells the time
of the cruel man
that lies in the house of Bedlam.

This is a world of books gone flat.
This is a Jew in a newspaper hat

that dances weeping down the ward
over the creaking sea of board
of the batty sailor
that winds his watch
that tells the time
of the busy man
that lies in the house of Bedlam.

This is a boy that pats the floor
to see if the world is there, is flat,
for the widowed Jew in the newspaper hat
that dances weeping down the ward
waltzing the length of a weaving board
by the silent sailor
that hears his watch
that ticks the time
of the tedious man
that lies in the house of Bedlam.

These are the years and the walls and the door
that shut on a boy that pats the floor
to feel if the world is there and flat.
This is a Jew in a newspaper hat
that dances joyfully down the ward
into the parting seas of board
past the staring sailor
that shakes his watch
that tells the time

of the poet, the man
that lies in the house of Bedlam.

This is the soldier home from the war.
These are the years and the walls and the door
that shut on a boy that pats the floor
to see if the world is round or flat.
This is a Jew in a newspaper hat
that dances carefully down the ward,
walking the plank of a coffin board
with the crazy sailor
that shows his watch
that tells the time
of the wretched man
that lies in the house of Bedlam.

# This Land Is Your Land

## Woody Guthrie
## (1912–1967)

*Considered the symbolic father of American folk music,
Guthrie captured the voice of the American people with his
honesty, humor, and fervor, exemplified here in his most famous and enduring creation.*

—m—

This land is your land
This land is my land
From California to the New York island
From the redwood forests to the Gulf Stream
       waters
This land was made for you and me.

As I was walking that ribbon of highway,
I saw above me that endless skyway:
I saw below me that golden valley:
This land was made for you and me.

I've roamed and rambled and I followed my
       footsteps
To the sparkling sands of her diamond
       deserts;
And all around me a voice was sounding:
This land was made for you and me.

When the sun came shining, and I was
    strolling,
And the wheat fields waving and the dust
    clouds rolling,
As the fog was lifting a voice was chanting:
This land was made for you and me.

As I went walking, I saw a sign there,
And on the sign it said "No Trespassing."
But on the other side it didn't say nothing,
That side was made for you and me.

In the shadow of the steeple I saw my people,
By the relief office I seen my people;
As they stood there hungry, I stood there
    asking
Is this land made for you and me?

Nobody living can ever stop me,
As I go walking that freedom highway;
Nobody living can ever make me turn back,
This land was made for you and me.

# Do Not Go Gentle into that Good Night

## DYLAN THOMAS
### (1914–1953)

*Though this poem is dedicated to and addresses Thomas's father, who was terminally ill at the time, it still resounds with the poet's characteristic imagery of natural beauty.*

—ᴍ—

Do not go gentle into that good night,
Old age should burn and rave at close of day;
Rage, rage against the dying of the light.

Though wise men at their end know dark is
    right,
Because their words had forked no lightning
    they
Do not go gentle into that good night.

Good men, the last wave by, crying how bright
Their frail deeds might have danced in a green
    bay,
Rage, rage against the dying of the light.

Wild men who caught and sang the sun in
    flight,
And learn, too late, they grieved it on its way,
Do not go gentle into that good night.

Grave men, near death, who see with blinding
  sight
Blind eyes could blaze like meteors and be
  gay,
Rage, rage against the dying of the light.

And you, my father, there on the sad height,
Curse, bless, me now with your fierce tears, I
  pray.
Do not go gentle into that good night.
Rage, rage against the dying of the light.

# A Supermarket in California

## ALLEN GINSBERG
## (1926–1997)

*A founder of the Beat movement, Ginsberg pictures himself encountering Walt Whitman, his poetic role model, as well as other legendary poets, in the aisles of a supermarket.*

—m—

What thoughts I have of you tonight, Walt
Whitman, for I walked down the sidestreets
under the trees with a headache self-
conscious looking at the full moon.
In my hungry fatigue, and shopping for
images, I went into the neon fruit supermarket,
dreaming of your enumerations!
What peaches and what penumbras! Whole
families shopping at night! Aisles full of
husbands! Wives in the avocados, babies in
the tomatoes!—and you, Garcia Lorca, what
were you doing down by the watermelons?

I saw you, Walt Whitman, childless, lonely old
grubber, poking among the meats in the
refrigerator and eyeing the grocery boys.
I heard you asking questions of each: Who
killed the pork chops? What price bananas?

Are you my Angel?
I wandered in and out of the brilliant stacks of
cans following you, and followed in my
imagination by the store detective.
We strode down the open corridors together in
our solitary fancy tasting artichokes,
possessing every frozen delicacy, and never
passing the cashier.

Where are we going, Walt Whitman? The
doors close in an hour. Which way does your
beard point tonight?
(I touch your book and dream of our odyssey
in the supermarket and feel absurd.)
Will we walk all night through solitary streets?
The trees add shade to shade, lights out in the
houses, we'll both be lonely.

Will we stroll dreaming of the lost America of
love past blue automobiles in driveways,
home to our silent cottage?
Ah, dear father, graybeard, lonely old courage-
teacher, what America did you have when
Charon quit poling his ferry and you got out on
a smoking bank and stood watching the boat
disappear on the black waters of Lethe?

# Wanting to Die

ANNE SEXTON
(1928–1974)

*Contemporary and friend to Sylvia Plath, Sexton wrote this poem to answer the question the world asked of Anne, Sylvia, and all suicidal people: "Why do you want to kill yourself?" Sadly, it now addresses our question: "Why did you?"*

—⚏—

Since you ask, most days I cannot remember.
I walk in my clothing, unmarked by that
        voyage.
Then the almost unnameable lust returns.

Even then I have nothing against life.
I know well the grass blades you mention,
the furniture you have placed under the sun.

But suicides have a special language.
Like carpenters they want to know *which*
        *tools.*
They never ask *why build.*

Twice I have so simply declared myself,
have possessed the enemy, eaten the enemy,
have taken on his craft, his magic.

In this way, heavy and thoughtful,
warmer than oil or water,
I have rested, drooling at the mouth-hole.

I did not think of my body at needle point.
Even the cornea and the leftover urine were
     gone.
Suicides have already betrayed the body.

Still-born, they don't always die,
but dazzled, they can't forget a drug so sweet
that even children would look on and smile.

To thrust all that life under your tongue!—
that, all by itself, becomes a passion.
Death's a sad Bone; bruised, you'd say,

and yet she waits for me, year after year,
to so delicately undo an old wound,
to empty my breath from its bad prison.

Balanced there, suicides sometimes meet,
raging at the fruit, a pumped-up moon,
leaving the bread they mistook for a kiss,

leaving the page of the book carelessly open,
something unsaid, the phone off the hook
and the love, whatever it was, an infection.

# Daddy

SYLVIA PLATH
(1932–1963)

*This work epitomizes the intense imagery and dark themes (often revolving around death and self-destruction) that haunt Plath's writing. Her father was a biology professor specializing in bees who died when she was eight years old.*

—⚡—

You do not do, you do not do
Any more, black shoe
In which I have lived like a foot
For thirty years, poor and white,
Barely daring to breathe or Achoo.

Daddy, I have had to kill you.
You died before I had time—
Marble-heavy, a bag full of God,
Ghastly statue with one gray toe
Big as a Frisco seal

And a head in the freakish Atlantic
Where it pours bean green over blue
In the waters of beautiful Nauset.
I used to pray to recover you.
Ach, du.

In the German tongue, in the Polish town
Scraped flat by the roller
Of wars, wars, wars.
But the name of the town is common.
My Polack friend

Says there are a dozen or two.
So I never could tell where you
Put your foot, your root,
I never could talk to you.
The tongue stuck in my jaw.

It stuck in a barb wire snare.
Ich, ich, ich, ich,
I could hardly speak.
I thought every German was you.
And the language obscene

An engine, an engine
Chuffing me off like a Jew.
A Jew to Dachau, Auschwitz, Belsen.
I began to talk like a Jew.
I think I may well be a Jew.

The snows of the Tyrol, the clear beer of
        Vienna
Are not very pure or true.
With my gypsy ancestress and my weird luck

And my Tarot pack and my Tarot pack
I may be a bit of a Jew.

I have always been scared of *you,*
With your Luftwaffe, your gobbledygoo.
And your neat mustache
And your Aryan eye, bright blue.
Panzer-man, panzer-man, O You—

Not God but a swastika
So black no sky could squeak through.
Every woman adores a Fascist,
The boot in the face, the brute
Brute heart of a brute like you.

You stand at the blackboard, daddy,
In the picture I have of you,
A cleft in your chin instead of your foot
But no less a devil for that, no not
And less the black man who

Bit my pretty red heart in two.
I was ten when they buried you.
At twenty I tried to die
And get back, back, back to you.
I thought even the bones would do.

But they pulled me out of the sack,
And they stuck me together with glue.

And then I knew what to do.
I made a model of you,
A man in black with a Meinkampf look

And a love of the rack and the screw.
And I said I do, I do.
So daddy, I'm finally through.
The black telephone's off at the root,
The voices just can't worm through.

If I've killed one man, I've killed two—
The vampire who said he was you
And drank my blood for a year,
Seven years, if you want to know.
Daddy, you can lie back now.

There's a stake in your fat black heart
And the villagers never liked you.
They are dancing and stamping on you.
They always *knew* it was you.
Daddy, daddy, you bastard, I'm through.

# Still I Rise

## MAYA ANGELOU
### (1928– )

*Angelou, who has read both at a presidential inauguration and at the Million Man March, is known for inspiring courage, perseverance, and self-acceptance. "Still I Rise" celebrates these themes, as well as her drive to be heard and to make a difference.*

—⚏—

You may write me down in history
With your bitter, twisted lies,
You may trod me in the very dirt
But still, like dust, I'll rise.

Does my sassiness upset you?
Why are you beset with gloom?
'Cause I walk like I've got oil wells
Pumping in my living room.

Just like moons and like suns,
With the certainty of tides,
Just like hopes springing high,
Still I'll rise.

Did you want to see me broken?
Bowed head and lowered eyes?

Shoulders falling down like teardrops.
Weakened by my soulful cries.

Does my haughtiness offend you?
Don't you take it awful hard
'Cause I laugh like I've got gold mines
Diggin' in my own back yard.

You may shoot me with your words,
You may cut me with your eyes,
You may kill me with your hatefulness,
But still, like air, I'll rise.

Does my sexiness upset you?
Does it come as a surprise
That I dance like I've got diamonds
At the meeting of my thighs? Out of the huts
      of history's shame
I rise
Up from a past that's rooted in pain
I rise
I'm a black ocean, leaping and wide,
Welling and swelling I bear in the tide.

Leaving behind nights of terror and fear
I rise

Into a daybreak that's wondrously clear
I rise

Bringing the gifts that my ancestors gave,
I am the dream and the hope of the slave.
I rise
I rise
I rise.

[Poem titles are in **boldface**]

243

# Acknowledgments

"Absence of the Soul 4" from "Lament for Ignacio Sanchez Mejias" from *Selected Verse* by Federico Garcia Lorca. Translation copyright © 1994 by Francisco Aragon, Catherine Brown, Cola Franzen, Will Kirkland, William Bryant Logan, Christopher Maurer, Jerome Rothenberg, Greg Simon, Alan S. Trueblood, John K. Walsh, and Steven F. White. Reprinted by permission of Farrar, Straus and Giroux, LLC.

"Ancient Music" by Ezra Pound, from *Personae.* Copyright © 1926 by Ezra Pound. Reprinted by permission of New Directions Publishing Corp.

"Buffalo Bill's" by E. E. Cummings. Copyright 1923, 1951, © 1991 by the trustees for the E. E. Cummings Trust. Copyright © 1976 by George James Firmage, from *Complete Poems: 1904–1962* by E. E. Cummings, edited by George J. Firmage. Used by permission of Liveright Publishing Corporation.

"Drinking Alone in the Moonlight" by Li Po, translated by Elling Eide, from *Poems by Li Po.* Reprinted by permission of the translator.